HOME REPAIR AND IMPROVEMENT

KITCHEN RENOVATIONS

OTHER PUBLICATIONS:

DO IT YOURSELF
The Time-Life Complete Gardener
The Art of Woodworking
Fix It Yourself

COOKING
Weight Watchers® Smart Choice Recipe Collection
Great Taste/Low Fat
Williams-Sonoma Kitchen Library

HISTORY
The American Story
Voices of the Civil War
The American Indians
Lost Civilizations
Mysteries of the Unknown
Time Frame
The Civil War
Cultural Atlas

TIME-LIFE KIDS
Library of First Questions and Answers
A Child's First Library of Learning
I Love Math
Nature Company Discoveries
Understanding Science & Nature

SCIENCE/NATURE
Voyage Through the Universe

For information on and a full description
of any of the Time-Life Books series listed above,
please call 1-800-621-7026 or write:

Reader Information
Time-Life Customer Service
P.O. Box C-32068
Richmond Virginia 23261-2068

HOME REPAIR AND IMPROVEMENT

KITCHEN RENOVATIONS

BY THE EDITORS OF TIME-LIFE BOOKS, ALEXANDRIA, VIRGINIA

The Consultants

Richard Day has been writing in the home-improvement field for 40 years and was a Home and Shop consulting editor for *Popular Science* magazine. A director and past-president of the National Association of Home and Workshop Writers, Mr. Day has written numerous articles and several books on concrete, masonry, and plumbing.

Stuart McLaughlin has been working in the design and renovation field for 17 years. Technically trained as a graphic artist, Mr. McLaughlin specializes in the design and layout of cabinets and built-ins.

Joe Teets is a master electrician/contractor. Currently in the Office of Adult and Community Education for the Fairfax County Public Schools, he has been involved in apprenticeship training since 1985.

CONTENTS

1 PLANNING A RENOVATION 6
- Mapping Out a New Kitchen 8
- Cabinets to Suit the Layout 14
- Setups for Special Needs 19

2 UPGRADING THE INFRASTRUCTURE 20
- Turning Off Water, Gas, and Electricity 22
- Clearing Out Space 24
- Removing Walls 26
- Preparing for a New Floor 33
- Exposing a Brick Wall 34
- Plumbing for Fixtures and Appliances 36
- Preparing for New Wiring 44
- Extending Circuits 48
- Putting in a Subpanel 59

3 WINDOWS, FLOORS, AND WALLS 62
- Opening a Wall for a New Window 64
- Adding a Counter-Level Window 68
- Creating a Wall of Natural Light 72
- Installing a Range Hood 75
- Laying a Floor of Ceramic Tiles 78
- Restoring Interior Walls 82
- Finishing With Trim Molding 90

4 CABINETS AND COUNTERTOPS 94
- Installing Stock Cabinets 96
- A New Work Surface 103
- Building Custom Frameless Cabinets 108
- Assembling and Hanging Cabinets 116

Index 126

Acknowledgments 128

Picture Credits 128

1

Planning a Renovation

One of the major benefits of renovating a kitchen is that you can tailor all its features to your needs and cooking style. Blending standard dimensions and layouts with the wealth of options in appliances, fixtures, and cabinets makes it possible to create a kitchen that is original and personal, as well as practical and easily accessed.

Mapping Out a New Kitchen   8

The Preparation Center
The Cooking Center
The Sink Center
Triangles That Save Time

Cabinets to Suit the Layout   14

A Collection of Cabinets
Sketching the Design

Setups For Special Needs   19

A kitchen layout →

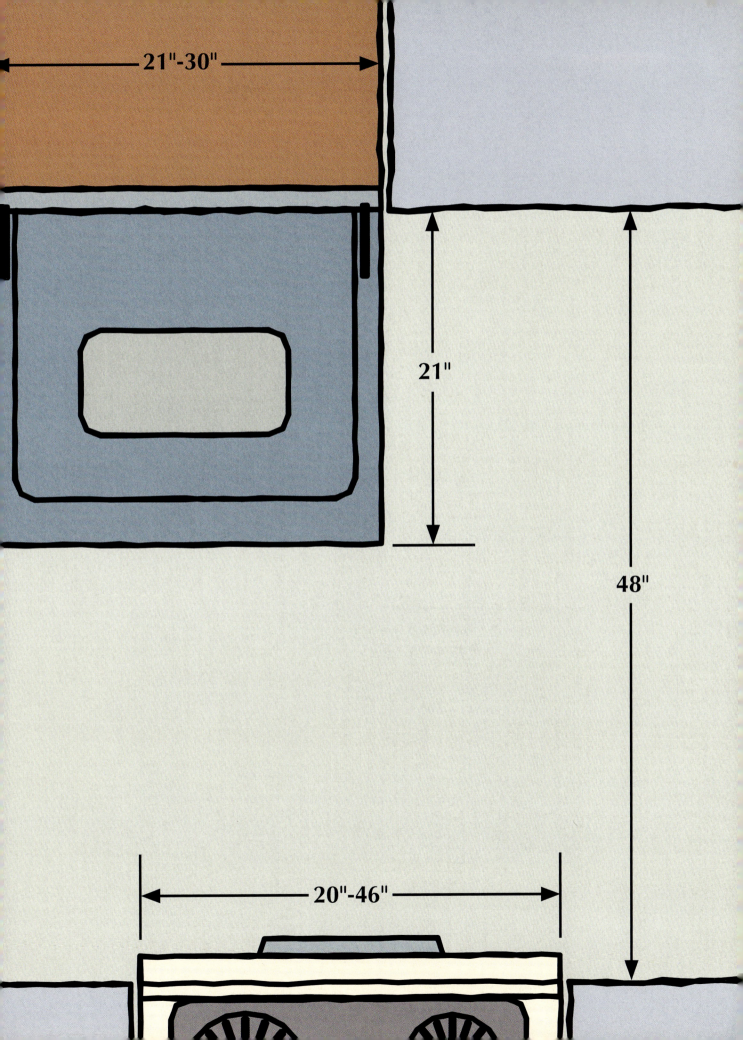

Mapping Out a New Kitchen

Above all, a kitchen is a culinary workshop. In designing for a renovation, you can plan the space to meet your personal tastes and cooking style.

Work Centers: Before laying out a design for a new kitchen, divide the room into three work centers, each containing work and storage space for a particular activity. The typical kitchen requires a preparation center, a cooking center, and a sink center *(pages 9-11)*. The measurements provided on these pages are standard across the home-building industry, but you can adjust any of the dimensions to tailor the kitchen to your needs.

Step-Saving Triangles: Cooks generally spend most of their time at the sink, stove, and refrigerator, and in traveling from one to the other. The most efficient way to arrange these components is in a triangle *(pages 12-13)*. Position the three elements so that the distance between each ranges from 4 to 9 feet, with the total of all three sides of the triangle equal to or less than 26 feet. Try to balance the desire for long counters against the need to keep the distance between the points of the triangle as short as possible—especially those converging on the sink, which is the most frequently used work center. Furthermore, design the kitchen so the triangle is isolated from house traffic as much as possible.

Kitchen Layout: As you consider a design, bear in mind these layouts: A straight kitchen has all the work areas on the same wall, so it requires ample room and generous amounts of space for work centers. A corridor or galley kitchen, set between two parallel walls, makes it easy to design an efficient work triangle, but traffic congestion may be a problem. An L-shaped kitchen is a functional design even in a limited amount of space. The compact and efficient U-shaped kitchen accommodates traffic well. An open-plan design, where no wall separates the kitchen from an adjoining family room, can be a center of activity as well as a space for cooking and eating. Such a kitchen requires a large room, or you can take down a wall separating two rooms to accommodate it *(pages 26-32)*.

Building Codes and Permits

Many kitchen renovation projects require a building permit. In addition, any work you do must comply with local codes. In most cases where a permit is needed, you will have to arrange for an inspection after the work is completed. Before embarking on your project, visit the building department in your municipality to determine whether you need a permit. Even if one is not required, you will have access to inexpensive advice from the professionals who work in the office.

The following types of projects generally require a permit:

◆ Structural changes such as the removal or addition of walls.
◆ Alterations to plumbing that involve rerouting drainage pipes.
◆ Electrical work such as upgrading a service panel.

THE PREPARATION CENTER

An overhead view.
In this preparation center, the counter is a minimum of 36 inches wide to accommodate ingredients, mixing bowls, and small appliances. Additional counter space at least 18 inches wide is required for an adjoining sink or major appliance. The counter here is 24 inches deep, but 16 inches is the bare minimum. With 60 inches of floor space, the kitchen allows for a 36-inch work zone at the floor—which accommodates open drawers—and a 24-inch traffic lane.

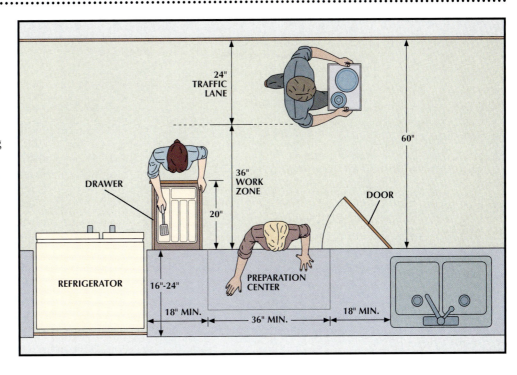

A side view.
At the preparation center, the countertop should be between 28 and 36 inches high; to customize this height for your stature, locate the counter 6 inches below your elbow when you are standing upright. Wall cabinets are placed at least 15 inches (18 inches on average) above base units—or 43 to 54 inches off the floor. Make sure the top shelf of a wall cabinet is no higher than 69 inches above the floor.

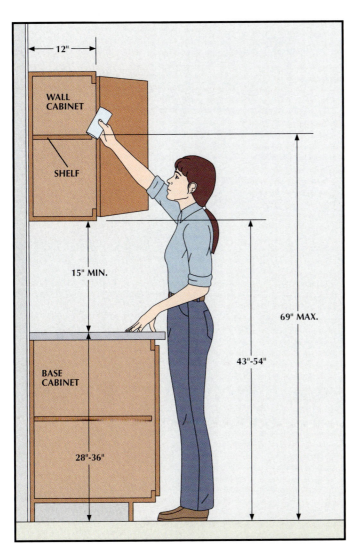

THE COOKING CENTER

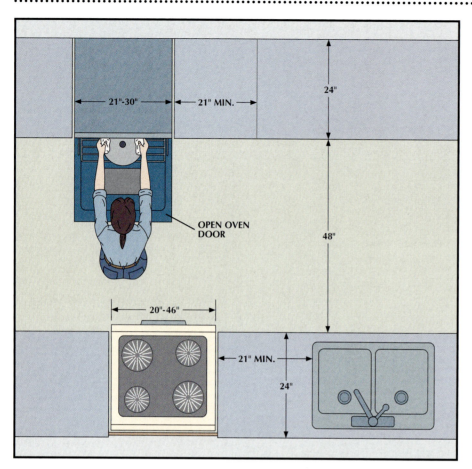

An overhead view.
The cooking center at left allows for at least 21 inches of countertop—ideally covered with a heat-resistant material such as ceramic tile—on each side of a cooktop that ranges from 20 to 46 inches wide. When there is a separate wall oven or microwave on the opposite wall, a minimum of 48 inches of floor space is required between obstructions to accommodate the cook and an open oven door.

A side view.
The top of a stove usually sits 36 inches above the floor; a separate cooktop set into a counter can be any height, but 34 inches from floor level is comfortable for most people. Because the typical exhaust hood extends $17\frac{1}{2}$ inches from the wall, a minimum of 24 inches of clearance between the burners and the bottom of the hood is necessary so the cook can see into tall pots. For a flammable surface such as the bottom of an upper cabinet, the space between that surface and the cooktop should be increased to 30 inches. Wall ovens should be mounted so the open door is about 4 inches below elbow height—an average of 36 inches from the floor.

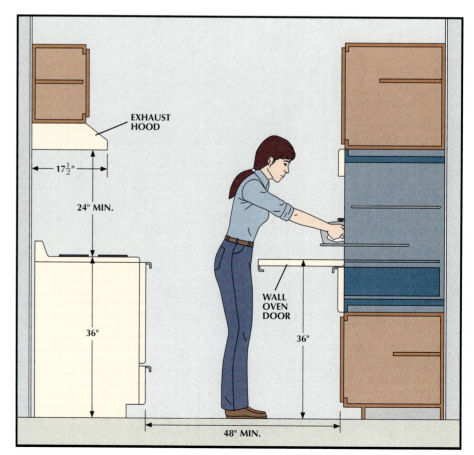

THE SINK CENTER

An overhead view.
In a sink center, the distance between the front of the sink and the front edge of the counter—known as the sink's setback—should not exceed 3 inches. At least 24 inches of counter space is required on one side of the sink for a dishwasher—18 inches for a rack of hand-washed dishes—and 36 inches on the other side for food preparation and cleanup. To accommodate the dishwasher's open door—the largest obstruction in the kitchen—a minimum of 54 inches of floor space is required between the counter and the nearest cabinet or wall, or 70 inches if traffic will have to pass in front of the door.

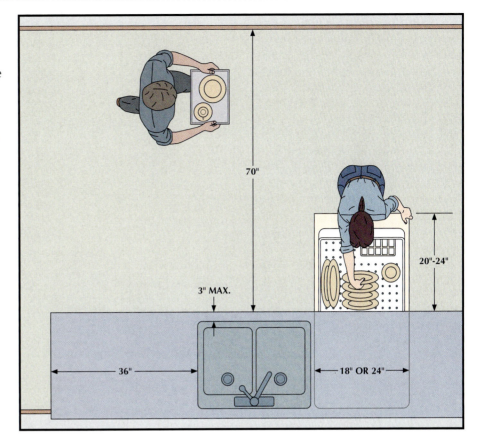

A side view.
Although the sink is usually installed at the same height as the countertop—typically 36 inches above the floor—for maximum comfort, the ideal height for the sink's rim is 2 inches below elbow height, or about 38 inches. A sink bowl 6 to 8 inches deep is ideal for most people; some models have a second, deeper bowl for washing large pots. Position wall cabinets at least 22 inches above the rim of the sink, with top shelves within 69 inches of the floor.

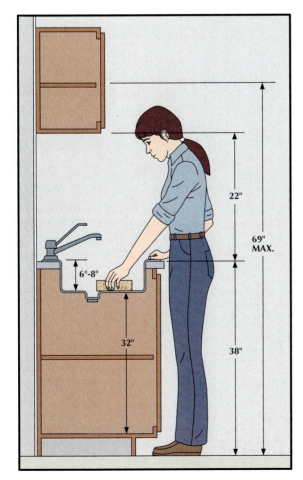

TRIANGLES THAT SAVE TIME

The galley kitchen.
The galley design is a workable arrangement where the long walls are at least 8 feet apart, leaving a 4-foot corridor when the cabinetry is installed; a 3-foot corridor is the absolute minimum for a work triangle of adequate size whose sides range in length between 4 and 9 feet. The stove and refrigerator are placed along one wall, facing the sink on the opposite wall. The dishwasher can be located on either side of the sink. This design is well suited to kitchens with a dead end at one of the short walls, since through traffic would result in congestion. A pantry can be installed on the dead-end wall.

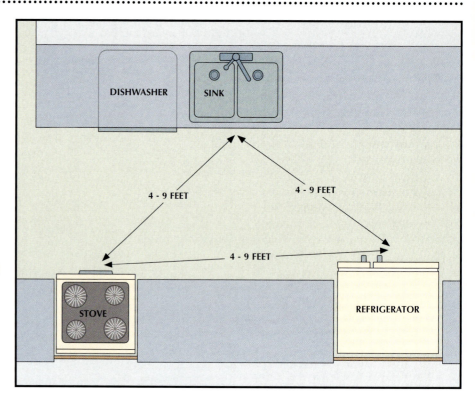

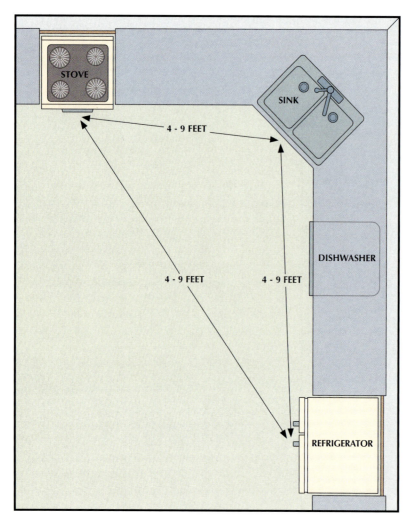

The L-shaped kitchen.
In a square room, the L kitchen places the sink at a corner, with the stove and refrigerator on adjacent walls, as shown at left; alternatively, two of the elements can be placed on one wall and the third on the adjoining wall. In either case, the work triangle is set in the corner, out of the way of traffic.

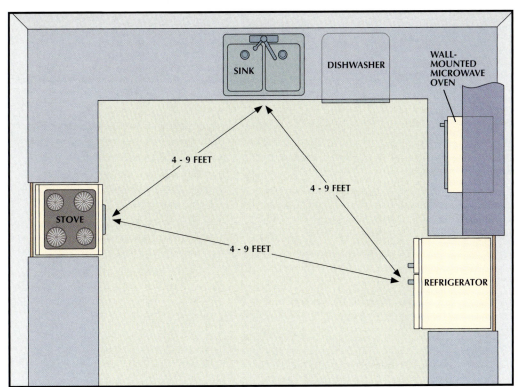

The U-shaped kitchen.
With the sink, stove, and refrigerator along three adjoining walls, the U kitchen allows for plenty of counter space and a compact work triangle. A fairly large kitchen is needed, however, with at least 5 feet of floor space between base cabinets on opposing walls. Where a microwave oven will be used primarily for defrosting and reheating foods, it is best situated beside the refrigerator.

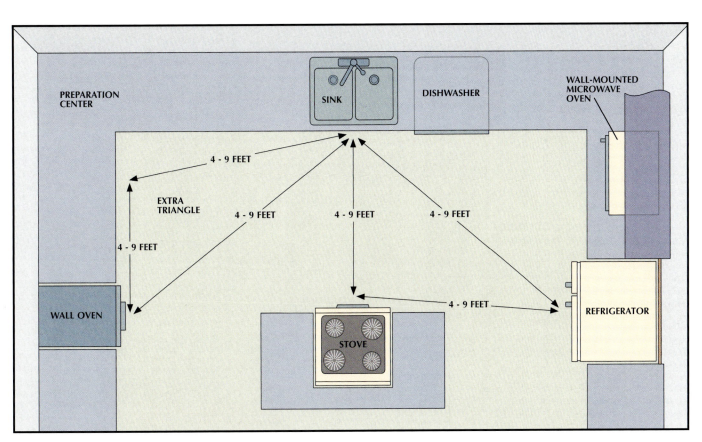

Adding extra triangles.
With enough floor space, the basic U kitchen can be supplemented by an island housing the stove and by a second work triangle. In this example, the second triangle encompasses the sink, a wall oven, and a preparation center. Since such triangles can have different appliances and purposes, their sides can range from 4 to 9 feet, provided the resulting area is compact and does not encroach on the primary triangle.

Cabinets to Suit the Layout

The abundance of kitchen cabinet designs and styles can be deceiving—most units are essentially just rectangular boxes. They may hold shelves, drawers, an oven, or a sink, and their proportions may change dramatically as their roles shift, but their consistency of shape makes them easy to arrange in layouts that suit varied needs.

Fitting Cabinets to the Space: As described in Chapter 4, you can buy cabinets ready-made, have them custom-made, or you can build them yourself. The units shown on the following pages are examples of some of the many configurations that are available. Cabinet sections are built in multiples of 3 inches in their width and depth, but because few kitchen walls are exact multiples of 3 inches or have perfect verticals meeting at true right-angled corners, cabinet manufacturers supply items called filler strips—sections of matching cabinet fronts that fill gaps where combinations of units do not exactly fit a wall, or where extra space is required to allow doors to open easily or to align the cabinets, doors, and drawers of upper and lower units. These strips—available both flat and as right angles—come in the same heights as wall and base cabinets and in widths of 3 or 6 inches, and can be sawed to narrower dimensions as needed.

To obtain an accurate placement of cabinets in your new kitchen, sketch the layout on a piece of graph paper, noting the positions and dimensions of the cabinets, along with any necessary filler strips *(pages 17-18)*. If the kitchen will be relatively small (under 150 square feet), sketch in base cabinets at least 21 inches deep with a combined width of 156 inches, and wall cabinets at least 12 inches deep and 30 inches high with a total width of 144 inches. For a larger kitchen, add 42 inches of base- and wall-cabinet width.

A COLLECTION OF CABINETS

Base cabinets.

Serving the dual purposes of storage and countertop support, base cabinets typically range between 30 and 38 inches high—stock cabinets are a standard $34\frac{1}{2}$ inches high—24 inches deep, and from 9 to 60 inches wide. All have a kick plate at the bottom to make working close to the countertop more comfortable. Standard base cabinets incorporate varying combinations of doors and drawers *(near right)* while other units are designed for special purposes. Double-door/sink cabinets have an open top for a sink, false drawers to blend with the rest of the cabinets, and double doors that allow easy access to plumbing and leave room for storage *(far right, top)*. A cabinet with double doors, reinforced rollout trays, and no center stile *(far right, bottom)* is useful for storing pots and pans.

DOUBLE-DOOR/DRAWER CABINET

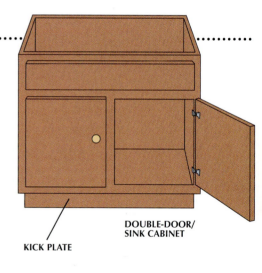

KICK PLATE

DOUBLE-DOOR/SINK CABINET

DOUBLE-DOOR/ROLLOUT TRAY CABINET

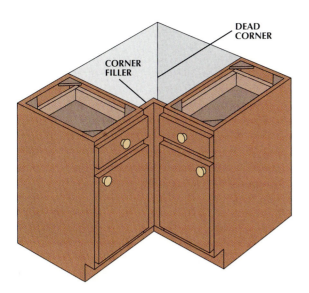
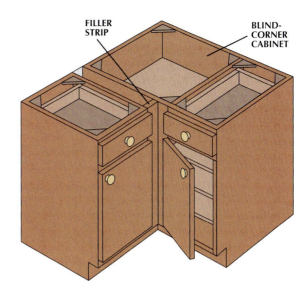
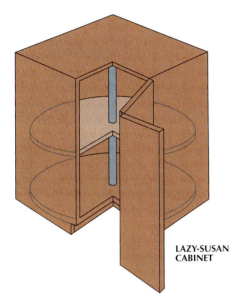

Options for corner base cabinets.

The simplest and least expensive way to deal with a corner is to link two cabinet runs with an L-shaped corner filler *(above, left)*. Called a dead corner, this option sacrifices considerable storage space since a large area is cut off from the cabinets. A blind-corner cabinet *(above, right)* solves this problem by extending into the corner and surrendering only a small area to a 3-inch-wide filler strip. Although this option allows most of the corner to be used for storage, items placed deep inside the unit may be difficult to reach. The most efficient way to use the space in a corner is with a lazy-susan cabinet *(left)*.

A VARIETY OF COUNTERTOPS

The countertop materials pictured below offer varying degrees of strength and durability, and are available in different price ranges. Some are easier to install than others. Plastic laminate *(far left)* is sturdy, inexpensive, and simple to apply, but its thin surface is difficult to repair. Impervious to heat and water, tile *(center, left)* comes in many colors and sizes. Solid-surface materials *(center, right)* are expensive but easy to install; and because they are made of a single material, pieces can be joined with almost invisible results. The most expensive material, granite *(far right)* is extremely hard and smooth, but also heavy and difficult to install.

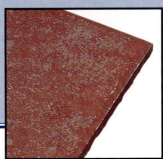

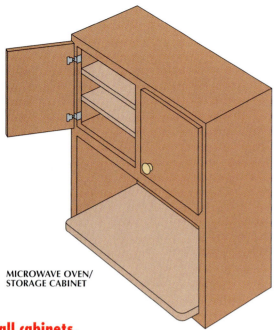

MICROWAVE OVEN/
STORAGE CABINET

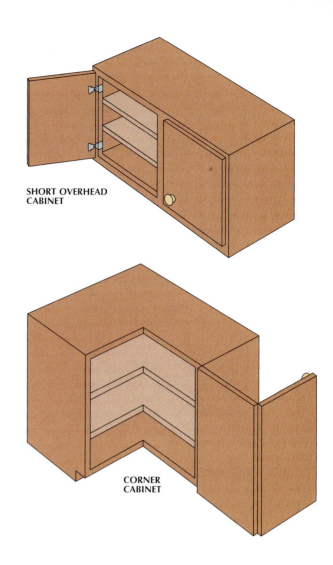

SHORT OVERHEAD CABINET

CORNER CABINET

Wall cabinets.
Cabinets fastened to the wall above the base units are typically 9 to 60 inches wide, 12 inches deep, and 12 to 30 inches high, with 30 inches being the standard height. Short versions of the standard cabinet are intended to be installed above a refrigerator *(above, right)*. A microwave-oven/double-door cabinet *(above, left)* holds the microwave and other items, freeing up counter space, while a double-hinged-door corner cabinet *(right)* allows you to make full use of corner space. A lazy-susan cabinet similar to the one shown on the previous page is also an option for making hard-to-reach wall corners more accessible.

Special-use cabinets.
Usually 84, 90, or 96 inches high, 24 inches deep, and variable in width, special-use cabinets can hold almost any combination of drawers, doors, and shelves. Designed to reach from the floor to the bottom of wall cabinets, these units can house an oven or serve as a broom closet or pantry.

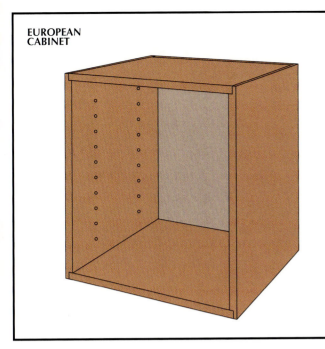

EUROPEAN CABINET

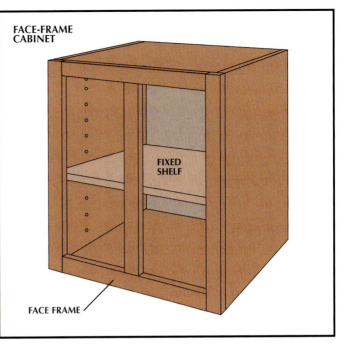

FACE-FRAME CABINET
FIXED SHELF
FACE FRAME

European and face-frame cabinets.
Kitchen cabinets are built in two basic styles: European and face-frame. Quick and easy to put together, Eurocabinets *(above, left, and pages 108-124)* are essentially frameless boxes. They owe their simplicity to the fact that all the holes in the pieces—whether for shelf-support pins, European hinges, or the screws and dowels that join panels—can be drilled using jigs to space them correctly on each piece. With a special system for hanging the cabinets on walls, the units can be installed efficiently—even by one person working alone. A face-frame cabinet *(above, right, and pages 96-102)*, constructed with a frame and a fixed shelf, is more rigid than a Eurocabinet. However, this type of cabinet is bulkier, making installation a little more difficult, and the face frames sometimes make it harder to get items in and out.

SKETCHING THE DESIGN

1. Drawing the top view.
◆ Tape a piece of tracing paper over a sheet of graph paper and mark the length and width of the room, letting each square of the graph represent 3 inches.
◆ Starting at a corner, lay out the positions of the base cabinets and appliances, centering the sink cabinet at a window and marking in the dimensions of each unit. Add filler strips where needed.
◆ Tape a second piece of tracing paper over the first and plot the wall cabinets.
◆ When the arrangement suits you, transfer the sketches to the graph paper *(right)*.

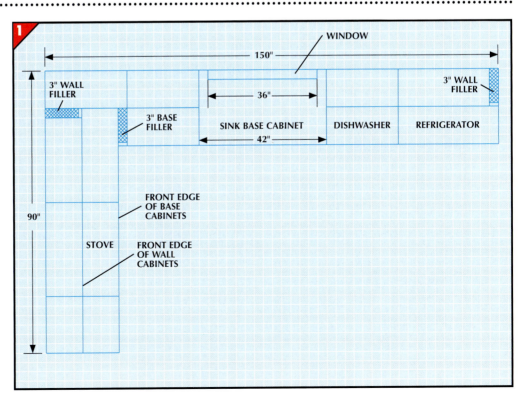

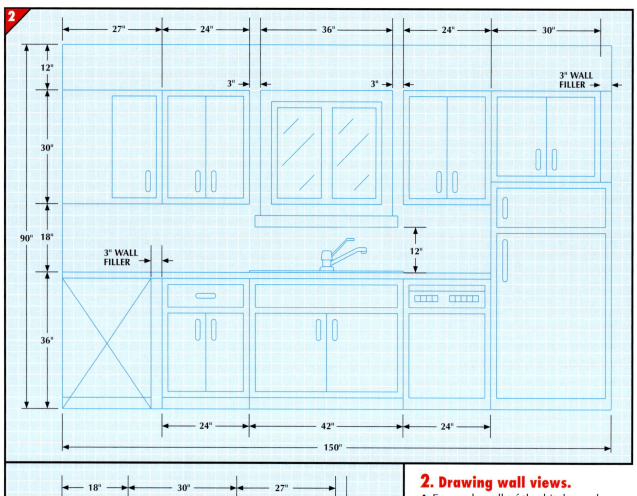

2. Drawing wall views.

◆ For each wall of the kitchen where you will be installing cabinets, tape a piece of tracing paper over a sheet of graph paper and, using the same scale as before, sketch in the cabinets. Include the doors and drawers, fillers, plumbing fixtures, and appliances; and mark the dimensions of the room and all the elements.

◆ Check the sketches to make sure the arrangement is visually pleasing, and that upper and lower cabinets, doors, and drawers are aligned.

◆ Transfer the views from the tracing paper to graph paper.

Setups For Special Needs

Designing a kitchen to accommodate a person with a disability can sometimes be accomplished with only slight modifications to the standard plan, such as altering the height or width of countertops. In other cases, more radical departures are called for.

Design Approaches: Special needs can be met in two basic ways. In one approach, most of the kitchen area follows standard dimensions, with selected work surfaces and storage spaces designed and positioned to be accessible to someone with special requirements. In a second approach, all cabinets and work surfaces are height-adjustable and so can be adapted to the needs of any kitchen user.

Work Surfaces: Countertops should be as continuous and unobstructed as possible. For cooks who need to work in a seated position, adequate knee space is required under the cooktop, sink, and preparation area.

Storage Space: For people with flexibility impairments or in a wheelchair, install shelves on roller glides rather than fixed shelving. You can also place under-counter cabinets on casters. To make wall cabinets accessible, position the lowest shelf no higher than 51 inches from the floor.

Fixtures and Appliances: Plan for a double sink 5 to 7 inches deep, with enough clearance underneath it for a wheelchair. A wall oven with side-hinged doors is easier to use than one with down-swinging doors, and a microwave oven on the counter is easier to reach than one in a wall cabinet. Every appliance should have a work area adjacent to it to aid in the handling and preparation of food.

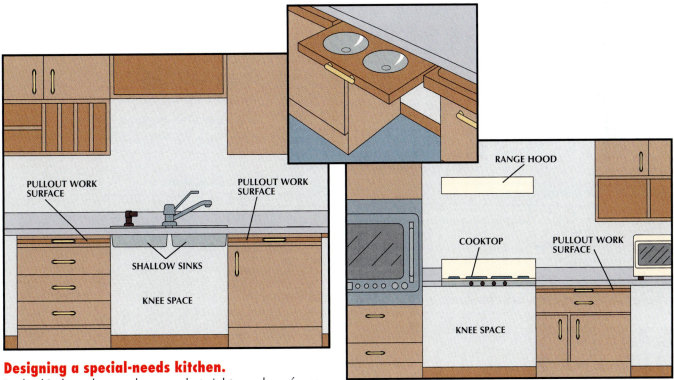

Designing a special-needs kitchen.
In the kitchen shown above and at right, work surfaces, storage areas, and appliances are readily accessible. At about 30 inches high, the countertop is lower than the standard and includes pullout work stations, some of which have removable bowls *(inset)* for convenient food preparation in a seated position. A cooktop with controls at the front allows a chair-bound person to use the appliance without having to reach over the burners. Under the cooktop and the shallow double sinks are large knee spaces. To accommodate a wheelchair, a knee space should be at least 27 inches high, 30 inches wide, and 10 inches deep. Recessed kick plates at least 8 inches high are needed at the base of cabinets to allow for the footrest of a wheelchair.

Upgrading the Infrastructure

A kitchen renovation generally entails a substantial amount of preparation before you can begin installing new flooring, cabinets, or appliances. Some of this activity may consist simply of removing old fixtures and appliances to clear the way for new ones. More involved procedures—like taking down a wall, rerouting plumbing lines, or running new electrical circuits—are sometimes necessary as well.

Turning Off Water, Gas, and Electricity   22
Stopping the Flow
Adding Shutoff Valves Under a Sink

Clearing Out Space   24

Removing Walls   26
Tearing Down a Nonbearing Wall
Leaving a Section in Place
Removing a Bearing Wall
A Strong Base for Header Support
Taking Out Part of a Bearing Wall

Preparing for a New Floor   33

Exposing a Brick Wall   34

Plumbing for Fixtures and Appliances   36
Tapping Into Supply Lines
A Layout for a New Sink
Hooking Up a Dishwasher
Bringing Water to a Refrigerator Ice Maker
Installing a Garbage Disposer

Preparing for New Wiring   44
Readying Cables for Connections
Joining Wires

Extending Circuits   48
Running Cable
Connecting to a Box
Wiring Receptacles
Hooking Up Single-Pole Switches
Three-Way Lighting Schemes
Installing Recessed Lighting in a Wallboard Ceiling
A Bar Hanger for a Heavy Ceiling Fixture

Putting In a Subpanel   59
Wiring the Box

Hooking up a dishwasher drain line →

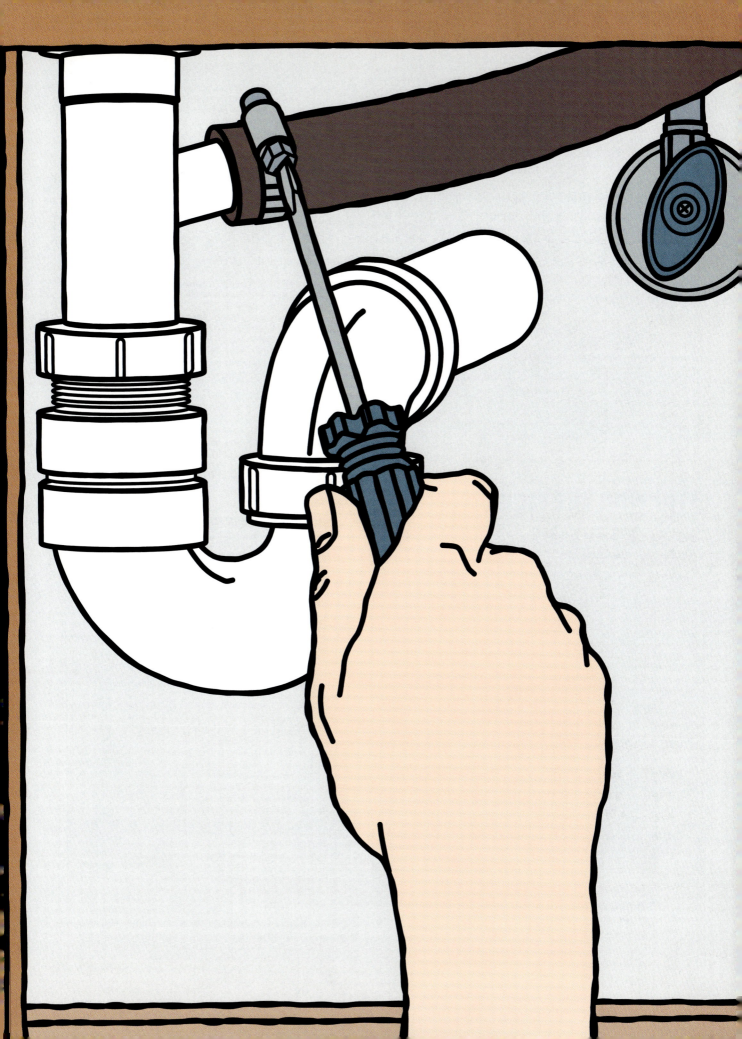

Turning Off Water, Gas, and Electricity

When you undertake a renovation project, you may need to disconnect and remove old fixtures and appliances. To do so, you will first need to turn off the electricity, gas, or water that supplies each item. Shut down electrical power to the kitchen circuits at the service panel *(below, left)*. Gas can generally be turned off at each appliance *(below, right)*. A fixture such as a sink may have valves underneath it that you can close; if it does not, you will have to turn off the water supply to the entire house *(opposite, top)*. Add shutoff valves before you reinstall the old fixture or put in a new one, so that it will be easier to repair or disconnect the fixture in the future *(opposite, bottom)*. If you will be soldering fittings to copper pipe, cover the wall behind the pipe with a flameproof pad, and keep a fire extinguisher nearby.

 TOOLS

Pipe cutter
Channel-joint pliers
Wire fitting brush
Adjustable wrench
Screwdriver
Propane torch

 **MATERIALS**

Plumber's abrasive sandcloth
Flux
Solder
Flameproof pad
Shutoff valves

 SAFETY TIPS

Wear goggles and gloves when you are soldering pipe.

STOPPING THE FLOW

Switching off electricity.
To cut power to each electrical circuit in the kitchen area, locate the breakers that control the circuits and switch them to the off position *(above)*. For a fuse-type panel, unscrew the fuses.

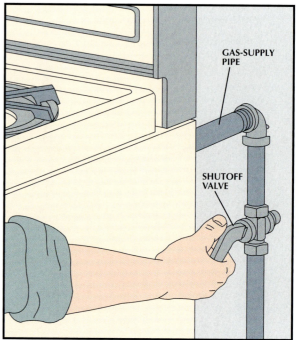

Closing the gas valve.
The shutoff valve for a gas appliance such as a stove is usually located on the supply line, close to the appliance. Turn the valve handle perpendicular to the pipe to shut off the gas *(above)*.

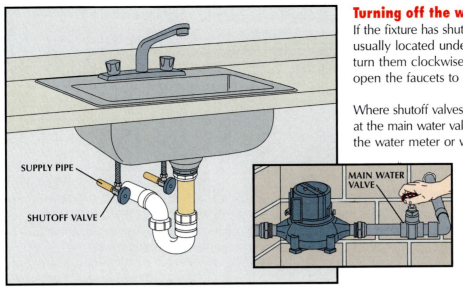

Turning off the water.
If the fixture has shutoff valves—at a sink they are usually located under the basin, as shown at left—turn them clockwise as far as they will go. Then open the faucets to confirm that the water is off.

Where shutoff valves are absent, turn off the water at the main water valve *(inset)*, usually located near the water meter or where the main water supply pipe enters the house. Drain the system by opening all faucets in the house, starting at the highest point and working down to the lowest.

ADDING SHUTOFF VALVES UNDER A SINK

1. Disconnecting the supply pipes.
◆ Turn off the water at the main valve and drain the system as described above.
◆ For copper pipe, sever each of the supply lines with a pipe cutter between the elbow and the wall *(right)*, cutting close to the elbow, then ream out the cut ends of the pipes with the triangular blade of the pipe cutter. If the pipes are made of galvanized steel, cut the vertical sections with a hacksaw about an inch above the elbows, then unscrew the elbows.
◆ Disconnect the drain lines and lift out the sink as described on page 24, Step 1.

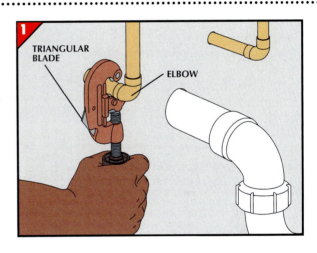

2. Installing the valves.
◆ On copper pipe, clean the cut pipe ends with plumber's sandcloth and brush a light coat of flux over the end of one pipe.
◆ Clean inside the socket of the shutoff valve with a wire fitting brush *(photograph)* and apply a coat of flux there.
◆ Open the valve fully, then slip it over the pipe.
◆ Play the flame of a propane torch on the pipe next to the valve. Keeping the flame away from the solder, touch solder to the joint, removing it when a bead of solder seals the seam. Install the other valve the same way *(left)*.

For steel pipe, wrap plumber's sealant tape around the threads of the pipes where you removed the elbows, then screw on the shutoff valves.

Clearing Out Space

The process of making way for a new kitchen begins with the removal of the old cabinets, fixtures, and appliances.

Fixtures and Appliances: Disconnecting a sink consists mainly of undoing nuts and fittings *(below)*. If there are no shutoff valves underneath, add them when you pull out the sink *(page 23)*.

You can sometimes leave freestanding appliances in place, but built-in ones—such as a cooktop or wall oven—will have to be moved. Turn off the gas or electricity to appliances before you do so *(page 22)*.

Cabinets: First take out the drawers and any adjustable shelves, then unscrew and lift off the countertop. You can remove doors from their hinges if you wish to make the cabinets easier to move. With the cabinets reduced to empty boxes, simply unfasten them from the wall *(opposite)*.

 TOOLS

Channel-joint pliers
Adjustable wrench
Basin wrench
Screwdriver
Pry bar
Reversible electric drill
Screwdriver bit

 SAFETY TIPS

Goggles will protect your eyes when using a power tool.

1. Disconnecting the sink.

◆ Turn off the water supply to the sink *(page 23)*.
◆ With channel-joint pliers, loosen the slip nut that connects the drain trap to the trap arm or the stub-out piece that comes straight out of the wall.
◆ Unscrew the slip nut holding the tailpiece to the sink drain and remove the washer and the tailpiece/drain trap assembly from the drain *(right)*.
◆ Detach the supply tubes from the shutoff valves with an adjustable wrench.
◆ Unscrew any clamps or lug bolts holding the sink to the counter, lift out the sink, and turn it upside down.
◆ With an adjustable wrench—or a basin wrench if the space is limited—detach the supply tubes from their faucet connections.

To reinstall the sink, reverse the procedure, but use a new tailpiece and drain trap instead of reconnecting the old ones.

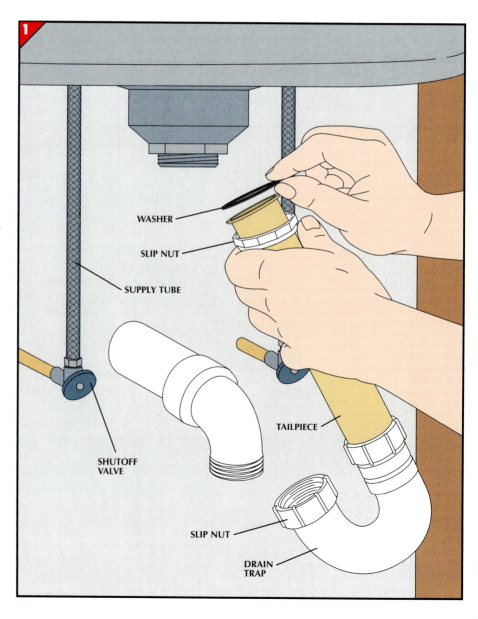

2. Removing the countertop.
◆ Take out the screws that anchor the countertop to the corner blocks attached to the cabinets *(left)*.
◆ If sections of the countertop are joined together, loosen the fasteners securing the seams.
◆ Working with a helper, if necessary, lift the countertop off the cabinets. If it won't move, it may have been glued to the cabinet—use a pry bar to lever it up from the base.

3. Detaching the cabinets.
◆ Starting with the base cabinets, remove any screws that hold adjacent units together; screws are typically driven through the sides of the stiles of the cabinet frames.
◆ Take out the screws that anchor the cabinet mounting rails to the wall *(above, left)*.
◆ Repeat the process for the upper cabinets *(above, right)*, working with a helper to lower the units to the floor.

Removing Walls

Enlarging a kitchen or creating space for a new one may entail tearing down one or more walls. Before you start, identify any complications by inspecting the wall.

Dealing with Utilities: Look for evidence of utilities inside the wall. Wiring that terminates at outlets there can be removed as you work *(opposite)*. Heating ducts, sometimes detectable from the basement or attic, can be cut back to the floor or ceiling and capped with a register. Pipes from an upstairs bathroom or from a hot-water heating system may need to be rerouted by a professional. For a wall with a large number of pipes and wires, you may be able to leave a section in place *(pages 28-29)* and have a professional move the utilities into the remaining section.

Bearing and Nonbearing Walls: Before you begin the job, determine whether the wall bears weight from above, thus serving as a vital structural element of the house *(below)*. Where you have any doubts, call in a professional, or simply assume that it is a bearing wall.

Removing a nonbearing wall *(opposite and pages 28-29)* is a straightforward demolition job, but a bearing wall *(pages 29-32)* can't be brought down without first supporting the weight it carries. To accomplish this, temporary shoring is erected on both sides of the wall and a header made of laminated veneer lumber (LVL) is installed along the ceiling. A lumber dealer can advise you on the correct width of the LVL, depending on the height and length of the wall and the floor it is on. To determine the proper length, measure the distance the header must span—including the thickness of any wall surfaces—and add $3\frac{1}{2}$ inches for each end where it intersects a perpendicular wall.

For walls greater than 14 feet long, or those with an especially heavy load above—a bathroom with a concrete floor, for instance—you may not be able to remove the structure. Even if the load is average, you need to determine that the posts supporting the header will rest on a solid structure *(page 31)*. If you have any doubts, have an engineer check your plans.

Finishing the Job: After the structure is removed, you'll need to patch breaks in the side walls and in the ceiling *(pages 82-89)*. The floor under the old wall can be built up with the same material as the existing finish floor.

TOOLS	
Pry bar	Mallet
Electronic stud finder	Hammer
Circular saw	Handsaw
Screwdriver	Staple gun
Wood chisel	Saber saw
	Carpenter's level
	Electric drill
	Combination bit

MATERIALS
Drop cloths
Polyethylene sheeting
Wallboard repair materials
Flooring materials
1 x 4s, 2 x 4s, 4 x 4s
Joist-dimension lumber
LVL board for header
Plywood for subfloor
Plywood ($\frac{1}{4}$")
Common nails (3", $3\frac{1}{2}$")
Carpet strip
Shims
Lag screws ($\frac{3}{8}$" x 5")

SAFETY TIPS

Wear goggles, work gloves, long sleeves and pants, and sturdy shoes when taking down a wall. Add a dust mask and a cap when cutting into a wall with a power tool.

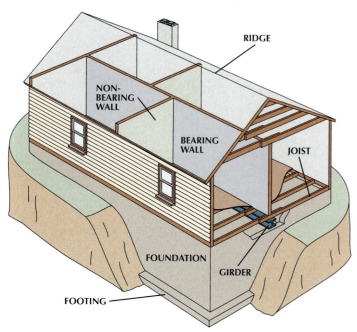

Bearing and nonbearing walls.
In a typical frame house, the roof is supported by the walls that run parallel to the ridge. The weight of the remaining structure—as well as the contents of the house—rest on joists, which transfer the load to the side walls. These walls pass the load to the foundation and footing. End walls usually do not carry weight. Since a standard wood joist may not span the usual distance from one side wall to another, house framers often use two joists and rest their inside ends on an interior bearing wall that carries the weight down to either another bearing wall that rests on its own footings or, as shown at left, to a girder whose ends rest on the foundation. Nonbearing walls generally run parallel to the joists and perpendicular to the roof ridge. To determine the joist direction, check the attic or basement, where joists are often exposed; if none are visible, cut a small hole at an inconspicuous spot in the ceiling.

CAUTION

Asbestos and Lead

Before 1978, lead was used in paint, while asbestos was found in wallboard, joint compound, resilient flooring, and insulation. Before cutting into walls or floors, mist the area with a solution of 1 teaspoon of low-sudsing detergent per quart of water, then cut out a small sample with a hand tool. Use a home test kit to check for lead; for asbestos, take samples to a certified lab. If either substance is present, you may want to hire a professional for the job; if you do the work yourself, follow these procedures:

! Keep people and pets out of the work area.

! Wear protective clothing (available from a safety equipment store) and a dual-cartridge respirator with high-efficiency particulate air (HEPA) filters. Remove the clothing before leaving the work area, wash the items separately, and shower immediately.

! Indoors, seal off work-area openings, including windows, doors, vents, and air conditioners, with 6-mil polyethylene sheeting and duct tape. Cover nonremovable items with sheeting and tape, and turn off forced-air heating and cooling systems.

! Never sand or cut material with power tools—mist them with detergent and remove them with a hand tool.

! Mop the area twice when the job is done. Place all debris in a 6-mil polyethylene bag and call your health department or environmental protection agency for disposal guidelines.

TEARING DOWN A NONBEARING WALL

1. Stripping the wall.
◆ Turn off power to the area at the service panel *(page 22)*.
◆ Cover the floor with drop cloths and tape polyethylene sheeting over doorways, windows, and vents.
◆ Remove the wall trim with a pry bar.
◆ Locate the studs on one side of the wall with an electronic stud finder, then cut strips of wall from between the studs with a circular saw set to the thickness of the wall surface; for a plaster-and-metal-lath wall, use a metal-cutting blade.
◆ Saw the studs in two near the middle and have a helper work them free from the top plate and soleplate *(above)*.

2. Removing wires.
◆ When you reach an outlet, remove its cover plate and take off the wall covering surrounding it.
◆ If the box is connected to a single cable coming up from a basement directly beneath, disconnect the cable from its receptacle and box, then tug on it while a helper watches from the basement to identify its origin *(above)*.
◆ Trace the cable to the nearest electrical box, disconnect it, and pull it out of the wall. If you cannot determine the cable's origin, if the outlet box has more than one cable entering it, or if unrelated cables pass through the wall, call in an electrician.

3. Removing the end studs.
◆ Loosen the bottom of one end stud with a pry bar, placing a wide wood scrap against the adjoining wall to serve as a fulcrum and protect the surface.
◆ Gradually work your way up the stud, continuing to loosen it.
◆ When the stud is safely away from the wall, wrench it free *(left)*.
◆ Beginning at the nailhead nearest one end, pry down the top plate, which is often nailed upward to blocks between adjacent joists. Use a wood scrap to protect the ceiling surface.
◆ Remove the other end stud in the same way.

4. Prying up the soleplate.
◆ Near the middle of the soleplate, make two cuts about 2 inches apart with a circular or reciprocating saw.
◆ Chisel out the wood between the cuts down to the subfloor.
◆ Insert a pry bar and lever up one end of the soleplate *(above)*. With a scrap of 2-by-4 as a fulcrum, pry up the other end.
◆ Pull up the other half of the soleplate with the same method.
◆ Patch the walls and ceiling *(pages 82-89)*, then lay down new flooring.

LEAVING A SECTION IN PLACE

1. Securing the top plate.
◆ Find and mark the stud where you will stop demolition of the wall.
◆ Cut the wall surface and plates so they extend $1\frac{1}{2}$ inches beyond the designated stud, creating a pocket for a reinforcing stud *(Step 2)*, then take down the unwanted portion of the wall *(page 27 and above)*.
◆ Remove a section of the ceiling about 1 foot wide, centered on the upper end of the stud and running to the second joist on each side.
◆ With two 3-inch common nails per side, fasten a block of joist-dimension lumber between the joists on each side of the top plate, with the face of the block flush with the end of the plate *(right)*.
◆ Drive two nails up through the top-plate extension into the bottom edge of the block.

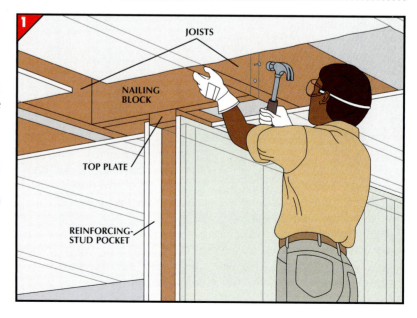

2. Fitting a reinforcing stud.

◆ Cut a 2-by-4 to fit snugly in the pocket between the top plate and soleplate, then fasten it to the end stud, driving 3-inch nails at 2-foot intervals *(right)*.
◆ Finish the outer face of the reinforcing stud with wallboard and corner bead *(pages 82-89)*.

REMOVING A BEARING WALL

1. Preparing the header.

◆ Mark notches at the upper corners of an LVL header 3 inches deep and $3\frac{1}{2}$ inches long, then, with a handsaw, cut the notches so the header will fit around the top plates in the adjoining walls *(left)*.
◆ Place the header on the floor against the wall to be removed so it will be inside the work space when the supports are erected.

2. Installing temporary supports.

◆ To hold up the ceiling until the header is in place, build support walls from 2-by-4s *(right)* or rent telescoping jacks *(photograph)*, positioning one at each end of the wall to brace a 2-by-10 beam against the ceiling.
◆ For a support wall, cut 2-by-4 top plates and soleplates about 4 inches shorter than the length of the wall to be removed.
◆ Cut studs $3\frac{1}{2}$ inches shorter than the distance from floor to ceiling and, with $3\frac{1}{2}$-inch common nails, fasten them to the top plate and soleplate at 16-inch intervals.
◆ Staple a strip of carpet to the top plate to protect the ceiling.
◆ Cut a strip of $\frac{1}{4}$-inch plywood as long as the soleplate and a bit wider, then position it about 30 inches from the wall. Raise the temporary wall onto the plywood strip and while a helper holds the wall in place, push shims firmly into the gap between the soleplate and the plywood strip.
◆ Brace the wall with a diagonal 1-by-4 nailed across the studs.
◆ Put up another temporary support wall on the other side of the wall, then remove the wall surface and studs *(pages 27-28, Steps 1-4)*.

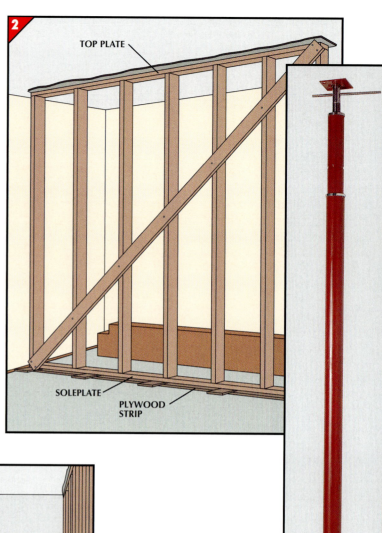

3. Prying out the plates.

The doubled top plate of a bearing wall is typically interlocked with that of the adjoining wall. Remove it as follows:
◆ Cut a 2-inch piece out of the middle of the plate with a saber saw, then pry a length down far enough to get a firm grasp of it. Work it free from the adjoining wall *(left)*.
◆ Remove the other section of the top plate in the same way.
◆ Cut and remove the soleplate *(page 28, Step 4)*.

A STRONG BASE FOR HEADER SUPPORT

1. Preparing the support posts.
◆ After the bearing wall has been removed, the breaks in the side walls will reveal nailer studs—pairs of close-set studs placed to provide a fastening surface for the wallboard.
◆ Cut the wallboard back to the nearest studs on each side of these nailer studs, then cut the nailer studs and pry them free *(right)*.
◆ Place the header, notched edge up, on the soleplates of the side walls at each end. Measure from the bottom of the notch to the joist above it and cut a pair of 4-by-4 posts to this length.
◆ With the header still on the floor, test-fit the posts to make sure they provide enough clearance for the notched ends of the header.
◆ To ensure sufficient support for the posts, first check the position of the soleplate by driving a nail through the floor next to it and locating the nail from the basement. If there is no girder or wall beneath the soleplate, consult an architect or contractor regarding proper placement of the header posts. Where the plate is located above a wall or girder but does not rest on a joist, install blocking to support the header posts: Cut two pieces of joist lumber long enough to fit between the joists and fasten them together with six 3-inch nails, then place them between the joists and secure their ends with two $3\frac{1}{2}$-inch nails *(inset)*.

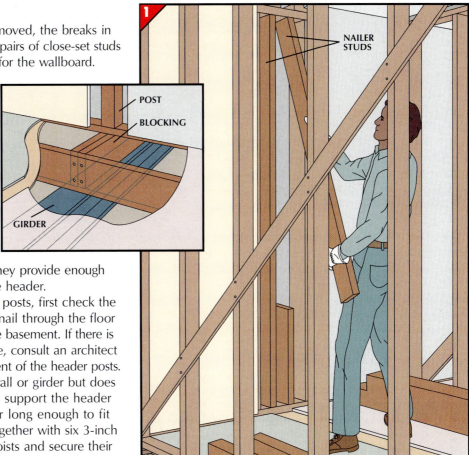

2. Raising the header.
◆ With a few helpers, lift the header to the ceiling and check whether it fits flush against the ceiling *(left)*. If any of the ceiling joists are low, put the header down and raise the sagging joists by adding shims beneath them on top of the temporary support walls.
◆ Raise the header again and while holding it in position, have helpers insert a post under each end. Check the posts with a carpenter's level to ensure they are plumb.
◆ Toenail the posts to the soleplate and the header with $3\frac{1}{2}$-inch nails.
◆ Remove the support walls.
◆ Patch the walls and cover the header with wallboard *(pages 82-89)*.

TAKING OUT PART OF A BEARING WALL

1. Preparing for support studs.
◆ To leave part of a bearing wall intact at both ends, start by setting up temporary support walls to span the planned opening *(page 30, Step 2)*.
◆ Dismantle the wall surface and studs back to the studs nearest the sides of the opening.
◆ Cut the doubled top plate flush with the stud at each end of the opening and remove it.
◆ Cut the soleplate $3\frac{1}{2}$ inches from the end studs and pry it from the floor *(page 28, Step 4)*, leaving an extension *(right)* to hold the support posts for the header.
◆ Determine whether the soleplate extensions stand over a joist or need the support of blocking *(page 31, Step 1 inset)*.

If you plan to leave only one end of a bearing wall in place, prepare the adjacent wall as on page 31, Step 1, leaving no part of the bearing wall's soleplate remaining at the end.

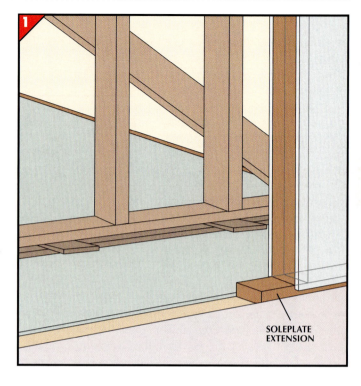

2. Raising the header.
◆ When part of the bearing wall remains intact at both ends, do not notch the header. Place the header on the soleplate extensions and measure the distance from the top of the header to the joist above it. Cut two 4-by-4 posts to this length.
◆ Raise the header, then insert a 4-by-4 post between it and the soleplate at each end.
◆ At four evenly spaced points along each post, drill counterbored holes through the post and adjacent stud, then join the post to the stud with $\frac{3}{8}$- by 5-inch lag screws and washers *(left)*.
◆ Cover the posts and header with wallboard *(pages 82-89)*.

If one end of the bearing wall is removed all the way to a side wall, cut a support post to fit into the side wall *(page 31, Step 1)*. Notch the end of the header that will abut the adjacent wall *(page 29, Step 1)* and attach the notched end to the support post *(page 31, Step 2)*.

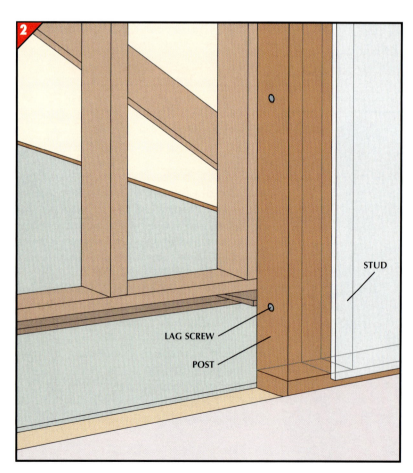

Preparing for a New Floor

Before you lay a new floor covering, check the condition of the subfloor; it may need repairing or replacing. If the floor feels soft or spongy, pull up the finish floor, then pry up the subfloor panels and lay new plywood of the same thickness *(below)*. When you will be installing ceramic tile *(pages 78-81)*, build up the thickness to $1\frac{1}{4}$ inches. Before you install the new plywood, check the floor joists. If they are more than 16 inches apart or consist of lumber smaller than 2-by-8s, have a carpenter reinforce them or install additional joists.

CAUTION: Resilient flooring that was installed prior to 1986 may contain asbestos; observe the precautions on page 27.

 TOOLS

Circular saw
Hammer
Electric drill
Wrench
Caulking gun

 **MATERIALS**

Plywood
2 x 4s
Construction adhesive
Ring-shank nails ($2\frac{1}{2}$")
Lag screws ($\frac{3}{8}$") and washers

Laying a new subfloor.

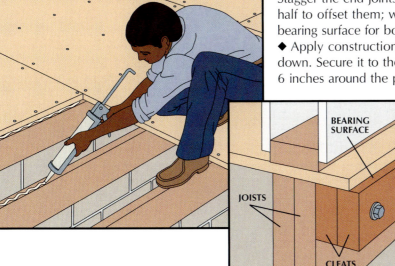

◆ Make a dry run, placing the sheets with their long edges perpendicular to the joists and leaving $\frac{1}{8}$ inch between sheets and along walls. Stagger the end joints between each row of panels, cutting sheets in half to offset them; where sheets meet a joist, make sure there is a bearing surface for both.
◆ Apply construction adhesive to the joists, then lay the first sheet down. Secure it to the joists with $2\frac{1}{2}$-inch ring-shank nails driven every 6 inches around the perimeter and every 12 inches in between. Install the remaining sheets in the same way *(left)*, staggering the nails along the edges with those in the adjacent sheet.
◆ Where floor joists are hidden beneath walls, add cleats as necessary to support the floor's outer edges: Nail one or more 2-by-4s to each concealed joist *(inset)* to provide at least a $\frac{1}{2}$-inch bearing surface. Secure the boards to the joists at 16-inch intervals with $\frac{3}{8}$-inch lag screws and washers.

Silencing a Squeaky Floor

To eliminate squeaks from a subfloor that is otherwise in good condition, shims may be the answer. If the subfloor is accessible from below, have a helper walk across the floor while you look for movement in the subfloor over the joists. To close these gaps, apply a bead of construction adhesive to both sides of the tapered edge of a wood shim and wedge it between the joist and the loose subfloor *(right)*, taking care not to force the subfloor upward.

Exposing a Brick Wall

Homes built before the 1940s may have some interior walls of brick that are concealed by plaster. Uncovering this brick in a kitchen can lend a rustic charm to the room. Remove a little plaster in a lower corner first to determine whether the brick is attractive enough to make the job worthwhile.

Dust Protection: The process of stripping away plaster will produce a great deal of dust. Before you start, empty cabinets and closets, and seal their doors—as well as heat returns and registers, and all doors leading out of the room—with masking tape. Protect the floor with $\frac{1}{8}$-inch-thick hardboard topped by plastic sheeting at least 4 mils thick.

Wiring: When the wall contains electrical boxes, disconnect the switches and receptacles, and remove the outlet boxes. If the electrical cables are old, you will need to run new wiring *(pages 44-61)*. Since the wires will run along the surface of the brick, instead of regular cable use armored cable (AC)—a flexible, metal type that protects the wires from damage.

Extra Touches: To match the color of the existing mortar for patching crumbling spots *(opposite)*, take a sample to a masonry supplier for a custom-tinted mix. Muriatic acid for cleaning bricks is available at paint stores, as are a variety of masonry sealers.

> **CAUTION** When cutting into walls, take precautions against releasing lead and asbestos particles into the air *(page 27)*.

TOOLS
Bricklayer's hammer
Wire brush
Cold chisel
Ball-peen hammer
Pointing trowel
Plastic bucket
Stiff-bristled brush
Caulking gun

MATERIALS
AC cable and clamps
Mortar mix
Muriatic acid
Masonry sealer
Silicone caulk

SAFETY TIPS

Wear goggles, a dual-cartridge respirator, and work gloves when you are breaking up a plaster wall. Switch to nitrile gloves when cleaning bricks with muriatic acid.

1. Breaking away plaster.
◆ Open windows in the work area to provide ventilation, and turn off power to any circuits in the wall *(page 22)*.
◆ Starting at the bottom of the wall, strike the plaster surface with a bricklayer's hammer at a 45-degree angle *(right)*. Pull cracked plaster away from the wall and strike succeeding hammer blows about 6 inches above the broken edge of plaster.
◆ With the chisel end of the hammer, chip off and pry out stubborn clumps of plaster.
◆ If the plaster has been laid over metal or wood lath, pry both the plaster and the lath off the wall.
◆ Remove any electrical cables, disconnecting them at the nearest electrical junctions.

2. Patching mortar joints.

◆ With a wire brush, remove any remaining plaster from the bricks *(left)*, then chip out loose mortar with a cold chisel and ball-peen hammer.
◆ Deepen the recesses for electrical boxes so that outlets and switches will be flush with the brick, and chisel out V-shaped grooves in the wall to accommodate runs of armored cable.
◆ Mix mortar and press it into the joints with a pointing trowel. Fill in gaps around door and window frames.
◆ Allow the mortar to set for 48 hours.

3. Cleaning the wall.

◆ Working with good ventilation, pour 1 part muriatic acid into a plastic bucket containing 3 parts water.
◆ With a stiff-bristled brush, apply the cleaning solution to the wall *(right)*. Try to avoid splashing; if acid spills on the plastic sheeting, blot it with newspaper.
◆ Rinse the wall by scrubbing it twice with fresh water.
◆ Let the wall dry for a week before proceeding.

> ⚠ **CAUTION** *Always pour acid into water, not the reverse. If your eyes or nose begin to sting while using the product, leave the room immediately.*

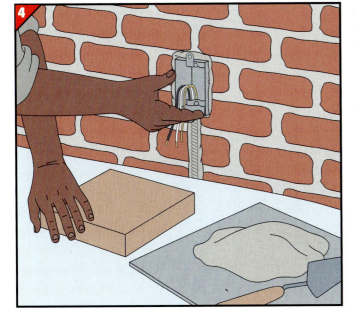

4. Rewiring and sealing the wall.

◆ Route AC cable from the service panel or nearby electrical junctions to the box locations, slipping it into each box and clamping it securely *(pages 44-61)*.
◆ Mortar the surfaces inside the electrical-box recesses, then push each box into place *(left)*. Press the cable into the grooves you cut in Step 2 and cover it with mortar.
◆ Scrape away excess mortar with the trowel, then press a board against the boxes to bring them flush with the wall.
◆ Let the mortar dry for 48 hours.
◆ Brush a coat of masonry sealer over the entire wall.
◆ When the sealer is dry, reconnect switches and receptacles *(pages 50-52)*, and replace the cover plates.
◆ Replace the baseboards and other pieces of wood trim that were removed.
◆ Caulk the joints between adjoining sections of brick and plaster wall, around door and window frames, and between the baseboard and the brick wall.

Plumbing for Fixtures and Appliances

When you renovate a kitchen, you may need to extend plumbing lines or hook up new fixtures and appliances. Before you begin, check local plumbing codes for guidelines and restrictions.

Pipe Materials: Supply lines usually are made of copper or a type of plastic called chlorinated polyvinyl chloride (CPVC). Copper is joined by soldering the parts together, while CPVC is glued using primer and cement. Drain lines typically are cast iron or another type of plastic—polyvinyl chloride (PVC). While PVC and CPVC are connected using the same techniques, they require different kinds of primer and cement.

You can extend plumbing lines with the existing pipe material, or you can change the material at the point where you tap into the old pipe. A copper supply line, for example, can be extended with plastic; it's also easy to mate plastic to cast iron.

In older houses, supply lines often were made of galvanized steel, which is joined with threaded fittings. To tap into this material, cut the steel pipe at the center of a short section and unscrew the fittings at each end. Screw new plastic adapters onto the exposed threads of the steel pipe and extend plastic lines from there; connect copper to steel in the same way, but use fittings called dielectric unions to prevent corrosion between the two dissimilar metals.

Laying Out the Plan: Determine the general location of the drain stack inside the wall by observing where it exits the roof, then pinpoint it with an electronic stud finder. Supply lines—often routed next to the stack—can sometimes be located with a stud finder as well. Position fixtures within a few feet of the stack, but do not add a connection for a new sink drain directly below a toilet connection. Make sure the new drainpipes slope properly—usually $\frac{1}{4}$ inch per horizontal foot—and that the lower end is not below the level of the water in the trap. New hot and cold supply lines should run about 6 inches apart. If cabinets will be installed over the plumbing, you can run the lines outside the wall surface *(opposite)*.

Hooking Up Appliances: Tubing for refrigerator ice makers can be put in either before or after the cabinets are installed *(page 41)*, while dishwashers *(pages 39-41)* and garbage disposers *(pages 42-43)* must be hooked up once the sink is in place.

 TOOLS

Pipe cutter　　　Ratchet pipe
Fitting brush　　　cutter
Propane torch　Screwdriver
Circular saw　　Wrench
Electric drill　　Hammer
Screwdriver bit　Putty knife
File

 **MATERIALS**

2 x 4s　　　　　PVC primer
Wood screws　　and cement
　($2\frac{1}{2}$" No. 8)　Plumbing-
Pipe and fittings　sealant tape
Plumber's　　　Stack clamps
　abrasive　　　Hubless bands
　sandcloth　　Shutoff valves
Flux　　　　　Flexible supply
Solder　　　　　line
CPVC primer　　Flexible drain
　and cement　　hose

 **SAFETY TIPS**

Put on goggles and work gloves when you are using a propane torch.

TAPPING INTO SUPPLY LINES

Branching off a copper line.
◆ Shut off the water supply to the house *(page 23)*.
◆ With a pipe cutter, cut the supply line at the point where you wish to extend it.
◆ As described on page 23, clean and prepare the pipes and fittings—in this case, a T-fitting instead of a shutoff valve.
◆ Slip the T-fitting over the cut ends of the pipe. If there is not enough play in the pipe run to do this, you may need to cut out a larger section of pipe and add a slip coupling and spacer as described on page 38, Step 3.
◆ Heat the joint with a propane torch. For tight spots, use a plumber's torch *(photograph)*. Solder the seam at one end of the fitting as described on page 23, then solder the other seam *(right)*.
◆ Extend pipe to the planned location by soldering a new length of copper pipe into the open end of the T-fitting.

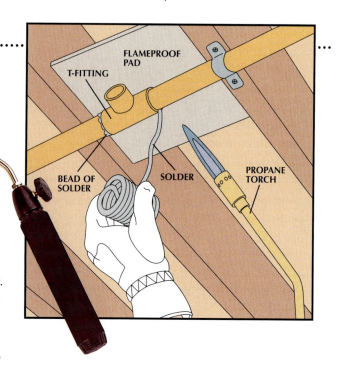

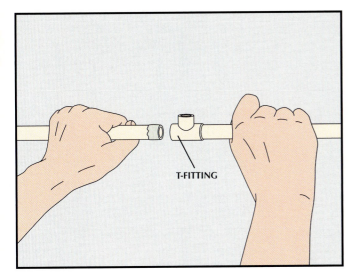

A connection in plastic pipe.
◆ Shut off the water supply to the house *(page 23)*.
◆ Cut the supply line with a pipe cutter, then trim off any burrs on the inside or outside of the cut ends with a knife.
◆ Apply CPVC primer to one end of the pipe and inside one end of a T-fitting.
◆ Coat the pipe end with solvent cement to a distance matching the depth of the coupling socket, then coat the inside of the socket.
◆ Push the fitting onto the pipe, give it a quarter-turn, and hold the pieces together for 10 seconds.
◆ Prime and cement the other socket and pipe end in the same way, then push the pieces together *(left)*. Wipe off excess cement with a clean, dry cloth.
◆ Extend pipe to the planned location by cementing additional CPVC pipe to the open end of the T-fitting.

Mating plastic to copper.
◆ Shut off the water supply to the house *(page 23)*.
◆ Solder a copper T-fitting to the cut pipe ends as described opposite, then solder a short length of copper pipe to the open end of the T.
◆ Disassemble a copper-to-CPVC adapter and solder its copper end to the open end of the pipe.
◆ Wrap plumbing-sealant tape around the threads of the adapter and screw the plastic end back on *(right)*.
◆ Extend pipe to the planned location by cementing additional CPVC pipe to the adapter as shown above.

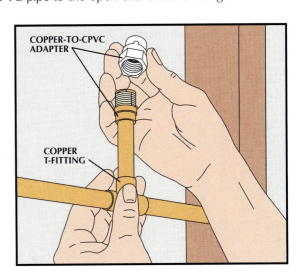

A LAYOUT FOR A NEW SINK

1. Roughing in.
◆ Locate the stack *(opposite)*.
◆ Make a vertical line representing the center of the new sink on the wall, then mark the trap 18 inches above the floor on the center line and supply lines 20 inches above the floor 4 to 6 inches on each side of the center line.
◆ Cut a hole between the studs flanking the stack and supply pipes, from just above the floor to the height of the supply-line extensions.
◆ Bolt stack clamps to the stack near the top and bottom of the opening, and support the ends with 2-by-4 cleats fastened to the studs with $2\frac{1}{2}$-inch No. 8 wood screws.
◆ Transfer the height of the trap center to the stack. To mark the position of the drain-line inlet on the stack, measure down from the mark $\frac{1}{4}$ inch for each foot of horizontal distance between the stack and the center line and make a mark there *(above)*.
◆ Make a drainpipe guideline between the trap mark on the center line and the drain-inlet mark on the stack.

CAUTION When cutting into walls, take precautions against releasing lead and asbestos particles into the air *(page 27)*.

2. Tapping into the stack.

◆ Using a plastic sanitary T the size of the stack but with an inlet that matches the size of the new drain line, align the T with the inlet mark on the stack (Step 1), then mark the top and bottom of the T on the stack.
◆ With a rented ratchet pipe cutter, cut through the stack 2 inches above the top mark and the same distance below the bottom mark.
◆ Slip a hubless band over the upper section of the stack and another over the lower portion.
◆ Cement a $3\frac{1}{2}$-inch-long piece of pipe as a spacer onto each end of the T.
◆ Slide the T into the gap in the stack, rotating it so it is oriented at a 45-degree angle to the wall, then slip the hubless bands over the spacers (right) and tighten the metal straps around the bands.

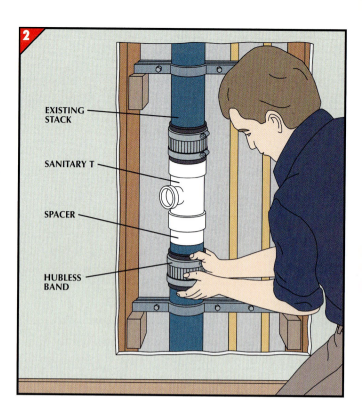

3. Adding supply Ts.

◆ Drain the water supply system (page 23).
◆ Cut an 8-inch section out of one supply line and, for copper pipe, solder a T (page 36) to the top piece and slide a slip coupling onto the lower one.
◆ Cut a spacer for the gap and fit it into the T (left). Slide the slip coupling onto the lower end of the spacer and solder it to seal the joint.
◆ Add a T to the other supply line in the same way.

For plastic pipe, cement (page 37, top) rather than solder the joints.

4. Getting outside the wall.

◆ On the supply-line Ts, solder (copper) or glue (plastic) short stubs of pipe that extend beyond the wallboard, then add 45-degree elbows.
◆ To the sanitary-T inlet, glue a short spacer of plastic pipe that extends just beyond the wallboard, then add a 45-degree elbow (right).
◆ Patch the wall (pages 82-89).

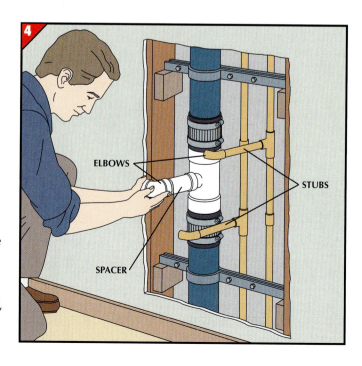

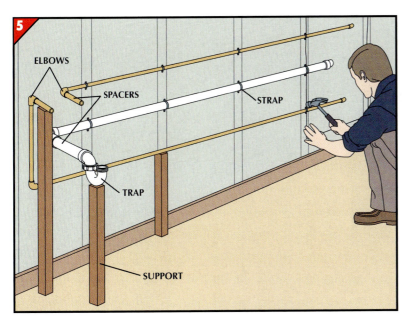

5. Anchoring the pipes.
◆ Loosely assemble the run of PVC drainpipe to reach the fixture location, supporting it with wood scraps.
◆ Attach a 90-degree elbow at the end and complete the assembly with a spacer, an elbow, and a trap—unless you will be adding a garbage disposer *(pages 42-43)*, where the trap is installed after the disposer is in place.
◆ Cement the joints and anchor the run of pipe with metal straps nailed to the studs.
◆ Install the supply pipes *(left)*, then add shutoff valves *(page 23)*.

TRICKS OF THE TRADE

A Pipe-Cutting Jig

Large enough to accommodate 3-inch-diameter pipe, the jig shown at right will help you make clean, square cuts in plastic pipe. Cut the base from a 2-by-4 and the sides from 1-by-4 lumber, and assemble the pieces into a U shape. Cut a kerf down the middle of the sides to the top of the base, ensuring that it is perpendicular with the base. To use the jig, place the pipe to be cut in it, aligning the cutting mark with the kerf; support the back end of the pipe with a 2-by-4 block. Install C-clamps on the sides at each end of the jig to hold the pipe steady. For smaller-diameter pipe, slip wood spacers between the sides of the jig and the pipe. Cut the pipe with a hacksaw.

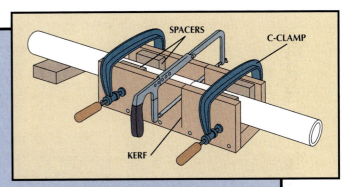

HOOKING UP A DISHWASHER

1. Connecting the hot-water line.
A dishwasher is connected to the hot-water line only; the job is usually performed after the cabinets and sink are in place *(Chapter 4)*.
◆ Turn off the water supply *(page 23)*.
◆ Install a T in the supply pipe *(pages 36-37)* where it exits the wall under the sink, add a short spacer pipe, then attach a shutoff valve *(page 23)*.
◆ Following the manufacturer's instructions, fasten a shutoff valve/coupling adapter for the dishwasher to the bottom of the T; then add a supply tube running from the shutoff valve to the sink faucet.
◆ Fasten one end of the dishwasher's supply hose to the adapter *(right)*. Attach the opposite end to the appliance—if necessary, routing it through a hole drilled in the cabinet next to the dishwasher.

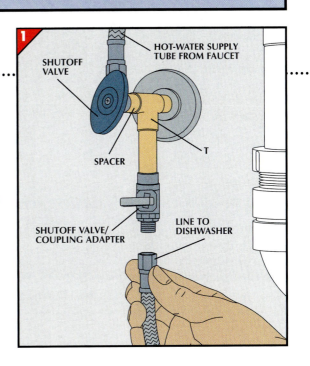

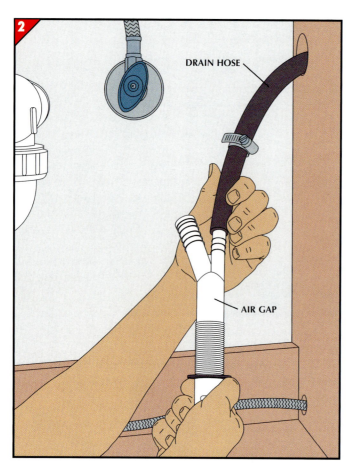

2. Installing an air gap.
◆ With an electric drill and a $2\frac{1}{4}$-inch hole saw, bore a hole through the countertop near the back edge between the sink and the dishwasher to accommodate the top of the air gap.
◆ Drill another hole through the side of the cabinet for the dishwasher's drain hose, fit the hose to one arm in the Y of an air gap inlet *(left)*, and secure the connection with a hose clamp.

3. Hooking up to the drain.
◆ Slip the air gap through the hole in the countertop so it extends above the counter by no more than $\frac{1}{2}$ inch, screw on the retaining nut, then cover it with its cap.
◆ Replace the sink drain's standard tailpiece *(page 24)* with a tailpiece adapter designed to link up with the air gap.
◆ Slip a length of 1-inch-diameter hose over the open ends on the air gap and the tailpiece adapter, then secure each connection with a hose clamp *(right)*.
◆ To connect the dishwasher wiring, run an electrical cable to the dishwasher's junction box *(pages 44-50)*, with enough slack to allow the appliance to be pulled out for servicing. Inside the box, attach the cable's black wire to the dishwasher's black wire with wire caps *(page 46)*, connect the two white wires using the same technique, and then join the two ground wires.

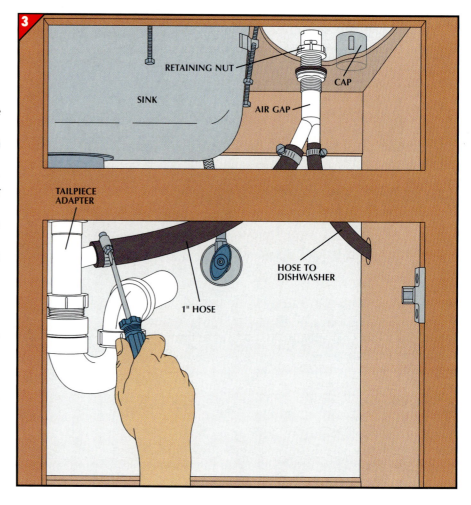

BRINGING WATER TO A REFRIGERATOR ICE MAKER

1. Installing a saddle shutoff valve.
◆ Turn off the water and drain the supply system *(page 23)*.
◆ Along the cold-water supply line close to the refrigerator's eventual location, drill a $\frac{1}{4}$-inch hole into the pipe. Remove any burrs with a file.
◆ Fasten the shutoff valve to the pipe with the pipe clamp supplied. Tighten the clamp screws just until the sealing washer begins to swell *(right)*.

CAUTION: *Avoid overtightening the clamp; doing so may crush the pipe.*

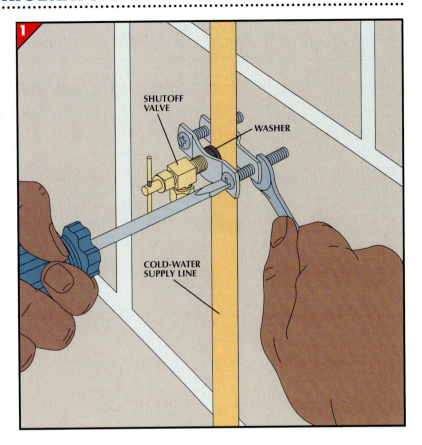

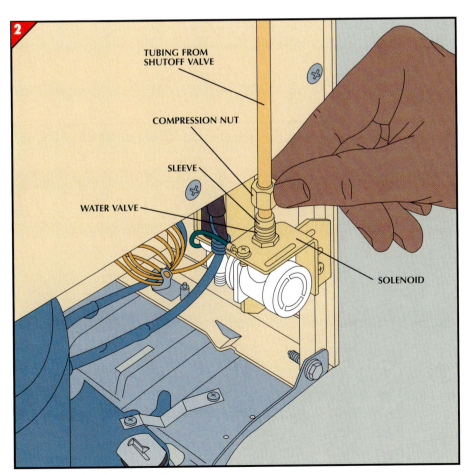

2. Running water to the fridge.
◆ Run a length of the flexible copper tubing supplied from the shutoff valve to the solenoid on the back of the refrigerator; drill holes through the cabinet sides, if needed, to run the tubing. For the model shown, take the dust cap off the water valve on the solenoid.
◆ Place the compression nut and ferrule sleeve supplied onto the end of the tubing.
◆ Insert the tubing into the water valve as far as possible, lower the sleeve over the connection, then slide down the nut *(left)* and tighten it with a wrench.

INSTALLING A GARBAGE DISPOSER

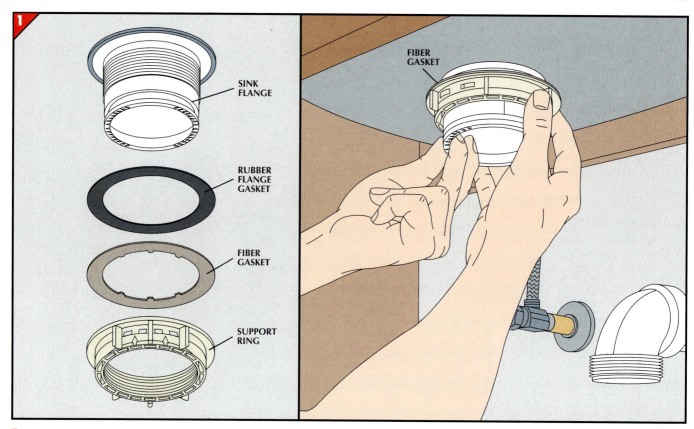

1. Securing the strainer.
The strainer assembly of a garbage disposer is comprised of four parts: a sink flange, a rubber flange gasket, a fiber gasket, and a support ring *(above, left)*.

◆ Remove the existing strainer assembly from the sink.
◆ With a putty knife, scrape any putty from around the drain hole in the sink.
◆ Set the rubber flange gasket supplied around the sink flange and, working from above, insert the sink flange into the sink opening.
◆ From under the sink, put the fiber gasket onto the sink flange and screw on the support ring by hand *(above, right)* until it is snug.

2. Preparing the disposer.
◆ Get the disposer ready for installation. For the model at right, seat the rubber gasket in the discharge port, slip the discharge elbow through its mounting bracket, and place it against the gasket.
◆ Fasten the elbow to the disposer using the screws supplied *(right)*.
◆ Note the location of the hopper projections around the outside rim at the top of the disposer.

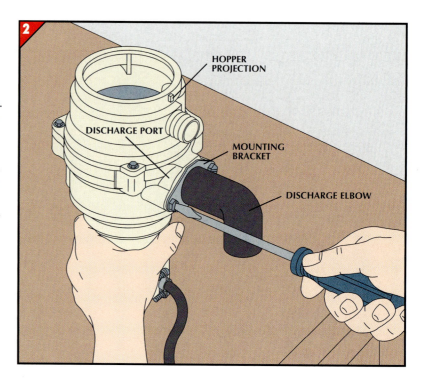

42

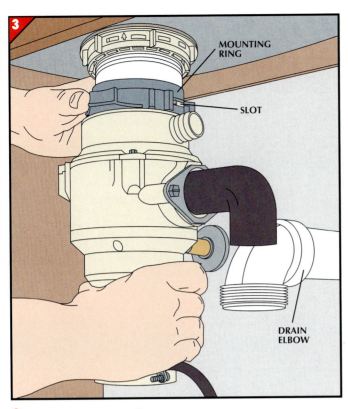
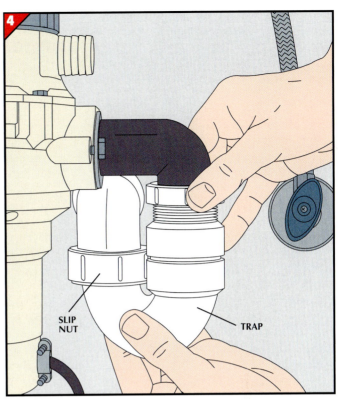

3. Mounting the unit.
◆ Holding the disposer under the strainer assembly, guide the hopper projections into their slots in the mounting ring; rotate the ring about $\frac{1}{4}$ inch clockwise to temporarily secure the unit.
◆ Rotate the mounting ring and disposer together until the waste outlet on the disposer's elbow lines up with the drain elbow.
◆ Holding the disposer steady, rotate the mounting ring until the hopper projections are at the extreme left of the mounting slots (above).

4. Hooking up the disposer to the drain.
◆ Fit a washer and slip nut onto the drain trap and fasten it to the drain elbow.
◆ Fit a slip nut onto the disposer's discharge elbow, insert a rubber washer into the trap, and slip the discharge elbow into the trap.
◆ Tighten the slip nut by hand (above).
◆ Restore the water supply, run water through the disposer, and check for leaks; tighten any loose connections.

WIRING A GARBAGE DISPOSER

To wire a disposer that has a power cord and plug, run a circuit from the electrical panel to an outlet box underneath the sink (pages 44-50) and hook up a combination switch-outlet (right): On the side of the switch-outlet that has two brass terminals, screw the cable's black wire to the terminal nearest the switch toggle, and break off the tab between the terminals with long-nose pliers. Fasten a black jumper wire between the two remaining brass terminals. Attach the cable's white wire to the silver terminal. Screw a green jumper wire to the switch's grounding terminal—for a metal box, add a jumper to the box's ground screw also—then cap the jumpers to the cable's ground wire (page 46).

For a disposer without a plug, run a cable from the electrical panel to a new switch location near the sink. Treat the switch as a middle-of-the-run switch (page 52), routing the outgoing cable to the disposer. Remove the disposer's junction-box cover plate, route the cable through the clamp, and cap together the black wires from the cable and disposer, then cap the white wires together. Attach the cable's ground wire to the disposer's grounding screw. Reattach the cover plate on the junction box and tape or tie the cable to the drainpipe to keep it out of the way.

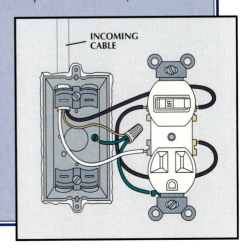

43

Preparing for New Wiring

Wiring for a new kitchen may consist simply of installing a few light fixtures or outlets, or it may entail running new circuits to the service panel or to a subpanel.

Before You Begin: Plan a wiring scheme according to the layout *(below)*, and determine the loads that will be placed on each circuit *(opposite, box)*. If existing circuits will be overloaded by additional electrical devices, install new cables and outlets *(pages 48-58)* and have an electrician hook them to new breakers on the service panel. Or, run additional circuits to a new subpanel placed near the kitchen—typically in the basement—connected by a single feeder cable to the main service panel *(pages 59-61)*. First, however, determine whether the service panel can handle the extra load. If it cannot, consult your electric company about increasing the power to your home, and have an electrician put in a larger panel.

Choosing Cable: The size of cable you need for each circuit depends on the application. For appliance circuits, use 12-gauge nonmetallic (NM) sheathed cable, rated to carry 20 amps. General lighting circuits *(pages 52-58)* use two-conductor or three-conductor 14-gauge NM cable providing 15 amps. An electric stove requires 6-gauge, three-conductor service-entrance round (SER) cable rated for 50 amps *(page 51)*.

Outlet Boxes: A variety of boxes are available for different uses *(page 47)*. If the wall or ceiling covering has not yet been installed, you can simply fasten the boxes to the exposed studs and ceiling joists. In finished rooms, however, you will need to cut holes in the wall covering to accommodate them. In these situations, mount the boxes at least 4 inches away from studs and joists to simplify running cable to them behind walls and ceilings.

 TOOLS

Cable ripper
Long-nose pliers
Lineman's pliers
Tin snips
Multipurpose tool

 **MATERIALS**

Electrical cable
Wire caps

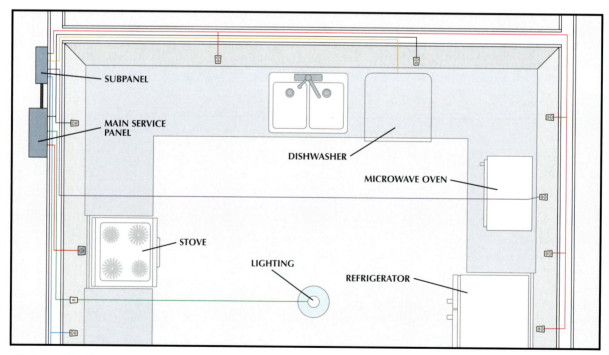

Kitchen circuits.

This fully-equipped kitchen has seven individual circuits, some of which are pre-existing and originate from the main service panel; the rest are hooked up to a new subpanel. The line for the electric stove *(red)* supplies 120 volts for the stove's light and clock, and 240 volts for its heating elements. Wiring for other major appliances—the dishwasher *(yellow)* and microwave oven *(purple)*—are separate 120-volt, 20-amp lines. Three 120-volt, 20-amp small-appliance circuits *(pink, black, blue)* supply the outlets, spaced no more than 4 feet apart. Also included is a 15-amp, 120-volt general lighting circuit *(green)*.

CAUTION

The Hazards of Aluminum Wiring

Between 1962 and 1972, nearly two million houses were wired with aluminum wiring. When connected to a dissimilar metal such as the copper-alloy terminals of a receptacle, the aluminum tends to corrode; and when the sheathing is removed, exposure to air causes the wire to oxidize. Both reactions increase the resistance in the wire, making it hotter when in use and therefore a fire hazard. Before you make any upgrades, check to see if you have aluminum wiring: the sheathing is marked AL, and the wire itself is dull gray. Never attempt to repair or improve a system with aluminum wiring, except for replacing switches or receptacles, and never try to install a ground-fault circuit interrupter (page 51). Exposed wire must be covered with a special antioxidizing paste; and all receptacles, switches, or other electrical devices must be the type marked CO/ALR. Any improvements must be in exact accordance with the National Electrical Code. Such work should be undertaken only by a licensed electrician.

CALCULATING LOADS

A circuit can be overloaded by too many appliances, particularly those that draw heavy wattage such as toasters. To determine how many devices each circuit can serve, first list every appliance or fixture that will be wired or plugged into it, together with the wattage they consume. Wattage is usually printed on light bulbs or on the data plates of appliances.

Calculate each circuit's continuous load (in amps) by adding up its total wattage, then dividing the result by 120 (the voltage). Check the service panel for the amperage that each circuit supplies, listed on its breaker or fuse. The continuous load should not exceed 80 percent of the circuit's capacity—16 amps on a 20-amp circuit, 12 amps on a 15-amp circuit.

READYING CABLES FOR CONNECTIONS

1. Removing cable sheathing.
◆ Cut a length of cable a couple of feet longer than you actually need to provide a margin for error. The excess can remain hidden inside the wall or ceiling.
◆ Make a 3-inch slit through the cable with a cable ripper or an electrician's knife. Avoid damaging the insulation on the wires inside—even a small nick can cause a short.
◆ Grasping the bare copper ground wire with long-nose pliers and holding the end of the cable with lineman's pliers, pull the wire through the sheathing to expose 10 to 12 inches *(right)*.
◆ Bend back the sheathing and cut it off with tin snips.

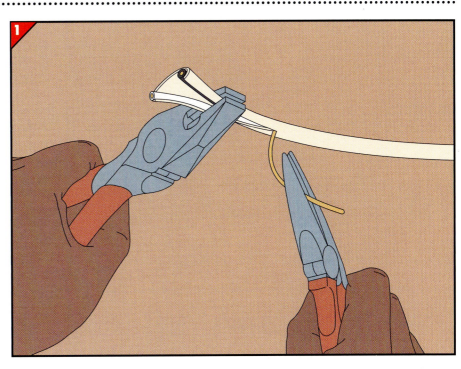

2. Stripping insulation.

◆ Match the gauge of the wire you are working with—it is embossed on the plastic sheathing of the cable—to the corresponding wire stripping hole in a multipurpose tool.
◆ Close the tool over one of the wires $\frac{1}{2}$ to $\frac{3}{4}$ inch from the end and rotate the tool a quarter-turn in each direction.
◆ Without opening the tool, pull the severed insulation off the wire to expose the bare metal.
◆ Strip the remaining wires in the same way *(right)*.

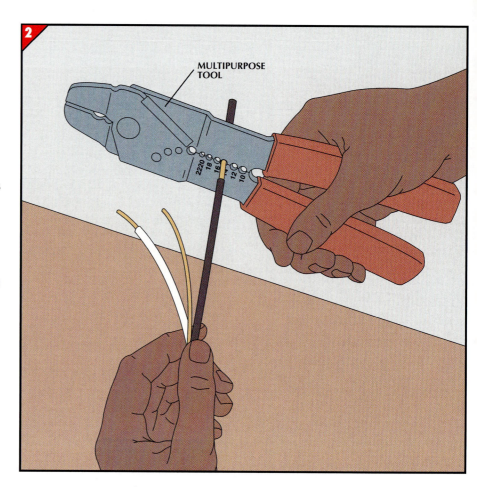

JOINING WIRES

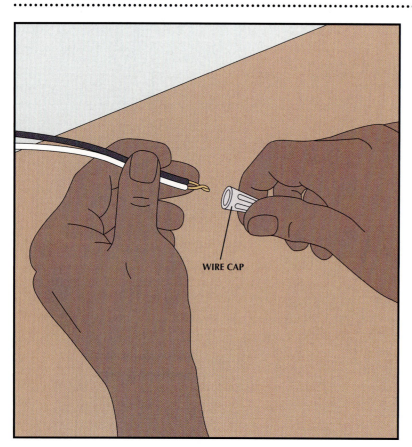

Connecting solid wire.
◆ After stripping the insulation from the wires, hold them next to each other with long-nose pliers and twist the exposed metal ends together clockwise with lineman's pliers.
◆ Place a wire cap over the twisted wires *(left)*. If bare metal is visible, remove the cap and trim the ends of the wires without untwisting them.
◆ Push the wires firmly into the base of the cap as you twist the cap clockwise until the connection is tight.

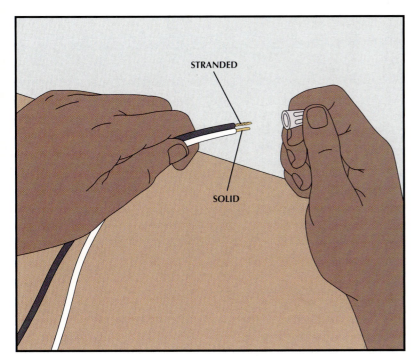

Connecting stranded wire.

◆ When connecting stranded wire to solid wire, strip about $\frac{1}{8}$ inch more insulation from the stranded wire than from the solid wire.

◆ Hold the two wires side by side as shown at left, then, without twisting the wires together, check the fit of a wire cap, making sure that it encloses every filament of the stranded wire.

◆ While pushing the wires firmly into the wire cap, twist it clockwise until the connection is tight.

A VARIETY OF BOXES

Outlet boxes provide structural support for switches, receptacles, and light fixtures, as well as protection for their wiring. They vary in shape according to their function and placement. Those that house receptacles, switches, and wall lights are almost always rectangular, while the ones for ceiling lights are octagonal or circular. Boxes also come in various sizes depending on the number of connections they will contain and the gauge of the wires. A wall box that will accommodate six connections with No. 12 wire, for example, must be at least $2\frac{3}{4}$ inches deep. Check with your electrical supplier for the right sizes for your project.

Boxes are held in place by different methods. If walls are unfinished, choose either plastic or metal boxes with flanges that can be nailed to studs. A flanged ceiling box nailed to a joist can support a 30-pound light, but where joists are inaccessible behind wallboard, a heavy fixture requires a ceiling box with a screw-type bar hanger (page 58). Plastic retrofit wall boxes have clamps at the top and bottom that lie flat against the box for insertion into an opening in a finished wall. As the screws are turned, the clamps rotate outward and pull the box tight against the wall covering. A metal retrofit box—also suitable for a finished wall—has a clamp that holds it securely against the back surface of the wallboard. On the type shown here, a screw inside the box is tightened to draw the clamps to the wall.

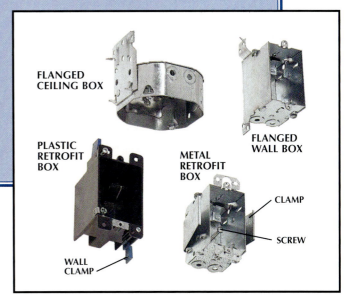

Extending Circuits

Putting in new circuits for a kitchen (page 44) involves running cable and installing outlets, as described on the following pages. If you are merely adding an outlet or two to an existing circuit, use the same techniques, but be sure that the power to the circuit is off before you begin work.

Fishing Cable to Boxes: When walls are unfinished, you can simply run cable through holes drilled in the center of each wall stud and into the boxes, then fasten the boxes to the studs (page 47, box). For finished walls, you will first need to cut holes at the planned locations of the boxes: Place a box on the wall at least 4 inches from wall studs, then trace its outline, ignoring the "ears" at the top and bottom of metal boxes or at the corners of plastic boxes. Cut along the outline with a wallboard saw. If the new subpanel will be located in an unfinished basement beneath the kitchen, feed the wire into the basement directly below the outlet box opening (below) and run it along the exposed framing members, stapling it at intervals no greater than $4\frac{1}{2}$ feet. For ceiling fixtures, use a similar technique to run cable through an attic above a kitchen. When you are extending a circuit or installing a subpanel in the kitchen, run the wire inside walls to the outlet or subpanel location (opposite).

Receptacles, Switches, and Lights: To minimize the hazards of operating appliances near water, a receptacle located within 6 feet of the kitchen sink must be a type known as a ground-fault circuit interrupter (GFCI) (page 51). Electric ranges call for a special outlet as well (page 51). For wall switches, you can choose between a single-pole switch (page 52) or a three-way switch (pages 53-55). Ceiling fixtures weighing 5 pounds or less can be hung from wallboard (pages 56-57), but heavier ones must be supported by a bar hanger (page 58).

CAUTION Before cutting into a wall or ceiling, check for the presence of lead and asbestos (page 27), and turn off electricity to existing circuits that run behind the wall or ceiling (page 22).

CAUTION If your house has aluminum wiring, follow the precautions on page 45.

 TOOLS
Electronic stud finder
Electric drill
Spade bit ($\frac{3}{4}$")
Fish tapes
Wallboard saw
Screwdriver
Tin snips
Socket wrench
Adjustable wrench

 **MATERIALS**
Electrical tape
Electric cable
Jumper wires
Wire caps
Outlet boxes
Receptacles
Switches
Recessed light fixture
Bar hanger

 SAFETY TIPS
Wear goggles while operating a power tool or when working overhead.

RUNNING CABLE

Fishing cable between floors.
◆ Drill a $\frac{1}{8}$-inch hole through the floor directly below the outlet-box opening, then poke a thin wire through the hole.
◆ Go to the basement and locate the hole; with a $\frac{3}{4}$-inch spade bit, bore a hole up through the soleplate next to it.
◆ Push the end of a fish tape (photograph) through the outlet opening, then have a helper in the basement push another fish tape up through the hole in the soleplate. Maneuver the tapes to hook their ends together (right).
◆ Pull the ends of the tapes through the outlet hole, then unhook them.
◆ Secure cable to the lower fish tape with electrical tape, then have your helper pull it into the basement and detach it from the fish tape.

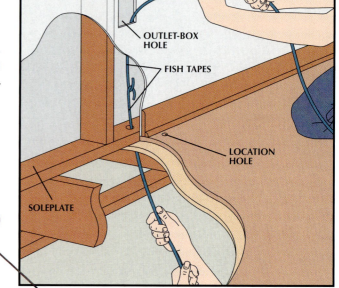

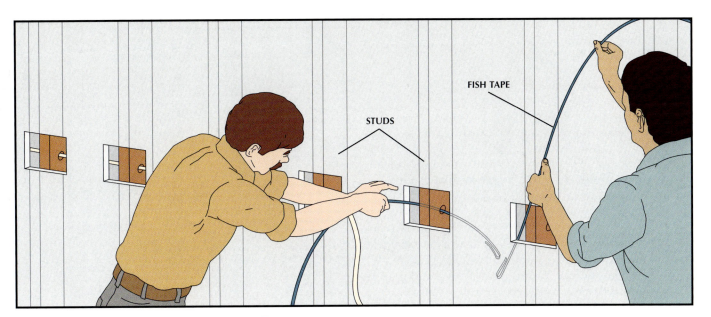

Running a circuit along a wall.
◆ With an electronic stud finder, locate and mark studs along the proposed path of the cable.
◆ Using a wallboard saw, cut a rectangular hole 3 inches high and 2 inches beyond both sides of each stud.
◆ Drill a hole through the center of each exposed stud with a $\frac{3}{4}$-inch spade bit.
◆ Feed a fish tape into the hole at one end of the cable run, then have a helper thread a second tape through the hole in the nearest stud.
◆ Hook the tapes together and pull the second tape out through the hole in the wall.
◆ Detach the tapes, fasten cable to the end of the second tape with electrical tape, then pull the fish tape and cable through the hole in the stud.
◆ Repeat this procedure *(above)* until you have reached the outlet box or subpanel location.
◆ Patch the wallboard *(pages 82-89)*.

CONNECTING TO A BOX

1. Preparing the outlet box.
◆ For a metal box, insert the tip of a screwdriver into the slot of a U-shaped knockout, pry the knockout away from the box, and work it free *(right)*.
◆ If the clamps inside the box are designed to accept either plastic-sheathed or armored cable *(photograph)*, the metal loops for armored cable must be removed for use with plastic-sheathed cable: Unscrew the clamp from the box, then use tin snips to cut the strips that connect the loops to the clamp, and discard the loops.
◆ Screw the clamp loosely in place.

With a plastic box, simply press on the clamp from the rear of the box to break the thin plastic or to engage the internal plastic clamps.

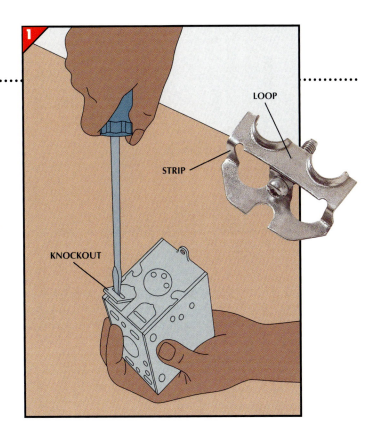

2. Clamping the cable.

◆ Strip the sheathing from the cable and wires *(pages 45-46)*, then pull the cable through the knockout hole and under the clamp so that at least $\frac{1}{8}$ inch of sheathing protrudes beyond the clamp.
◆ Screw the clamp tightly against the sheathed portion of the cable *(right)*, then attach the box to the wall *(page 47)*.

For a plastic box, strip the sheathing from the cable and wires *(pages 45-46)*, then push the wire under the flap on the outside of the clamp. Press the clamp against the sheathed portion of the cable. Attach the box to the wall *(page 47)*.

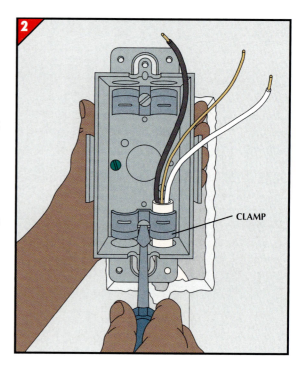

WIRING RECEPTACLES

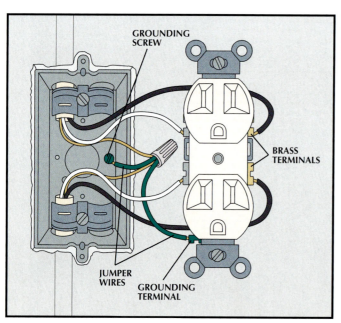

Middle of the run.
In the outlet at left, cable runs into it from the power source and then on to another outlet. The black wires of the two cables are fastened to the brass terminals of the receptacle and the white wires to the silver terminals. In this metal box, two short green jumper wires are employed to make the ground connection. One is fastened to the ground screw inside the box, and the other to the green grounding screw of the terminal. The two copper wires of the cables are joined to the free ends of the jumpers with a wire cap *(page 46)*. For a plastic box, connect the wires in the same manner, but omit the jumper to the box.

End of the run.
In an end-of-the-run outlet *(right)*, only one cable enters the box. In the metal box shown, the black wire is connected to either brass terminal of the receptacle and the white wire is fastened to either silver terminal. A short green jumper wire is attached to the green grounding screw of the terminal and another is fastened to the ground screw inside the box. The jumpers are joined to the copper ground wire of the cable with a wire cap *(page 46)*. In the case of a plastic box, the wires are connected in the same way, but the jumper to the box is omitted.

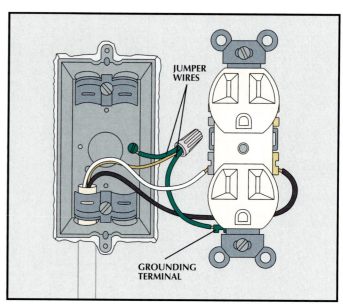

Wiring a GFCI.

The GFCI at right is a middle-of-the-run outlet *(opposite)*. In addition to affording protection at this receptacle, the GFCI protects all other outlets in the circuit downstream.

◆ To wire the GFCI, screw the black wire of the cable coming from the power source to the brass terminal labeled "LINE" and the corresponding white wire to the silver terminal marked "LINE."
◆ Hook up the outgoing cable in the same fashion, attaching its black and white wires to the terminals marked "LOAD."
◆ For the metal box shown here, fasten a green jumper wire to the GFCI's ground screw and another to the ground screw of the box. Join the jumpers and the copper wires of the cables with a wire cap *(page 46)*. For a plastic box, omit the jumper wire that connects the GFCI to the box.

If a GFCI is located at the end of a run *(opposite)*, fasten the black and white wires to the "LINE" terminals, and ground the outlet as for a middle-of-the-run receptacle.

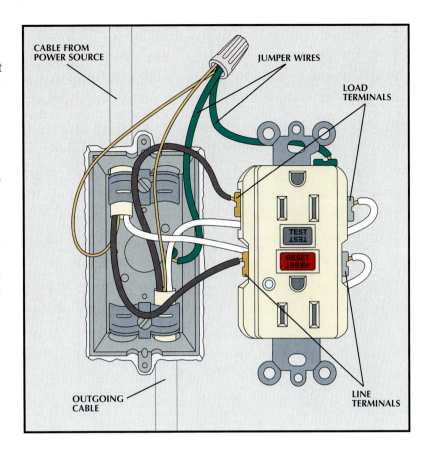

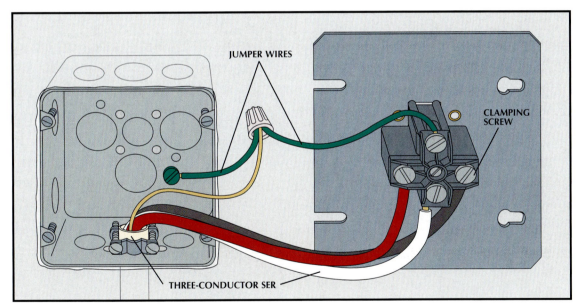

Wiring a range receptacle.

Fed by 6-gauge, three-conductor SER cable from the electrical panel, a 120/240-volt, 50-amp receptacle provides 240-volt current to the oven and elements of an electric range, as well as 120-volt current for the lights, timer, and other accessories.

◆ To wire the receptacle, insert a green jumper wire into the terminal marked "green," the white wire of the three-conductor cable into the terminal marked "white," and the red and black wires into the two remaining terminals.
◆ Tighten the clamping screw on each terminal.
◆ Fasten a green jumper wire to the ground screw of the box, then join both jumpers and the ground wire of the cable with a wire cap *(page 46)*.

HOOKING UP SINGLE-POLE SWITCHES

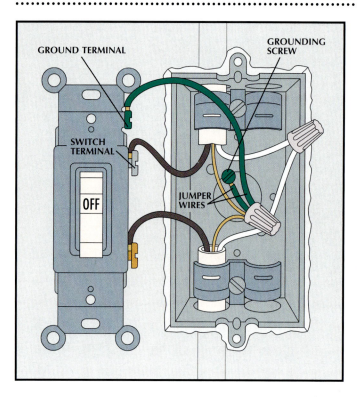

Middle of the run.
Nearly identical to a middle-of-the-run outlet *(page 50)*, a switch in this position receives power from a cable linked to the electrical source and controls power to a fixture or outlet downstream.
◆ To install the switch, attach the black wires from the incoming and outgoing cables to the terminals on the side of the switch.
◆ Join the white wires with a wire cap *(page 46)*.
◆ For the metal box shown here, attach green jumper wires to the switch's ground terminal and the ground screw in the box, then join the cables' bare copper wires to the two jumpers with a wire cap.

Wire a plastic box in the same manner, but omit the jumper to the outlet box.

A switch loop.
In this configuration, only one cable enters the box from the fixture. Since the black and white wires form a "loop" to the fixture and back, both serve as hot wires.
◆ Attach the black and white wires of the cable to the terminals on the side of the switch. For safety, recode the white wire as black with paint or a piece of electrical tape.
◆ For the metal box shown at right, add green jumper wires to the switch's ground terminal and to the ground terminal of the box, then join the jumpers to the copper wire of the cable with a wire cap *(page 46)*. In a plastic box, omit the jumper wires and fasten the cable's copper wire to the ground terminal of the switch.
◆ At the fixture, recode the white wire coming from the switch as black, and join the wires at the fixture in the same manner as those for the fixture in the three-way scheme opposite *(top inset)*.

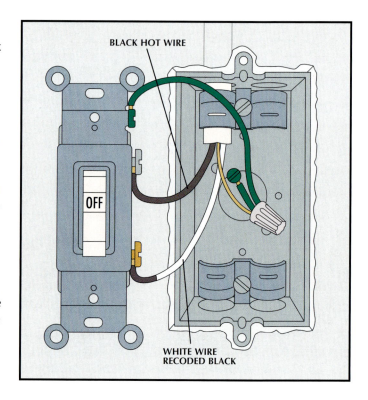

THREE-WAY LIGHTING SCHEMES

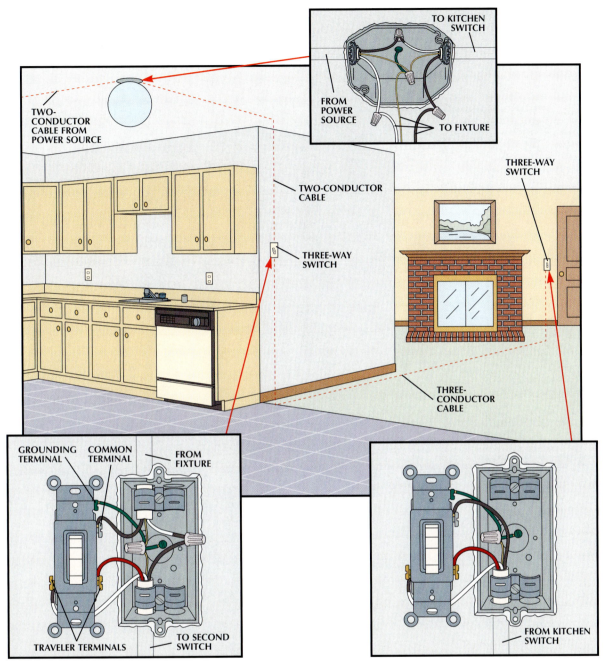

From light to switch to switch.
In this plan, two-conductor cable runs from the power source to the light fixture and from the fixture to the wall switch near the kitchen. Three-conductor cable travels from there to the switch in the adjoining room. The only neutral white wire is the one from the power source; all other white wires are part of a switch loop and therefore are recoded black.

◆ At the fixture, connect with wire caps *(page 46)* the incoming white wire to the fixture's white wire, the incoming black wire to the white wire of the outgoing cable (recoded black), and the outgoing black wire to the black fixture wire. Attach a green jumper wire to the box's grounding screw and fasten it to all the bare copper ground wires in a wire cap.

◆ At the kitchen wall switch, connect the recoded incoming white wire to the three-conductor cable's black wire, the incoming black wire to the switch's common terminal, and the outgoing red and white (recoded black) wires to the brass traveler terminals—those located at the bottom of the switch, directly opposite one another. Connect the bare copper ground wires and add jumper wires in the same way as for a middle-of-the-run switch *(opposite)*.

◆ At the switch in the adjacent room, connect the black wire of the cable coming from the kitchen switch to the common terminal, and the red wire and the white wire (recoded black) to the traveler terminals. Add jumper wires and join them to the bare copper wire as you would for a switch loop *(opposite)*.

53

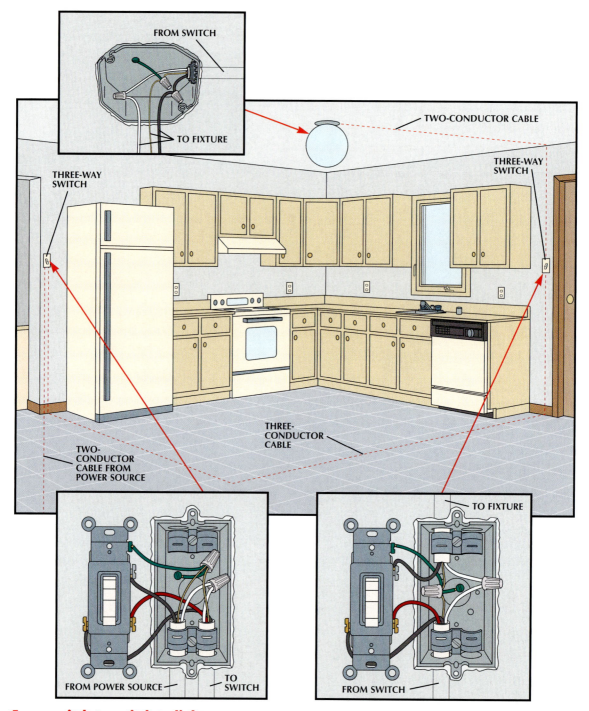

From switch to switch to light.

For a kitchen with two entrances, switches at either doorway control the light fixture. A two-conductor cable runs from the power source to the first three-way switch; a three-conductor cable then goes from the first to the second three-way switch; and finally, a two-conductor cable runs to the overhead light. In this circuit, the white wire in all three cables is neutral.

◆ At the first switch, join the two white wires with a wire cap *(page 46)*; connect the black wire coming from the power source to the switch's common terminal, and the outgoing black and red wires to the traveler terminals. Add jumper wires, and attach them and the bare copper wires in the same manner as for a middle-of-the-run switch *(page 52)*.

◆ At the second switch, connect the red and black wires coming from the first switch to the brass traveler terminals, join the white wires in a wire cap, and fasten the outgoing black wire to the common terminal. Ground the switch as you did the first one.

◆ At the light fixture, connect the cable's black wire to the fixture's black wire with a wire cap and join the white wires in the same way. Attach a short green jumper wire to the box and group it with the bare copper ground wires in a wire cap.

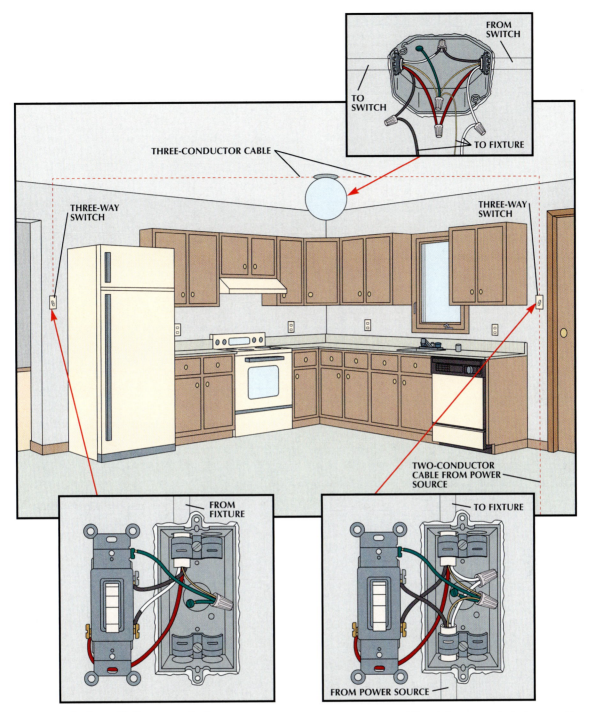

From switch to light to switch.

In this variation for wiring a kitchen with two entranceways, the power goes by two-conductor cable from the power source to the first switch, and by three-conductor cable from the first switch to the light fixture and on to the second switch. The white wire between the power source and light fixture is neutral; elsewhere it is used as a hot wire and accordingly recoded black.

◆ At the first switch, connect the incoming black wire to the common terminal, cap the two white wires *(page 46)*, and fasten the black and red wires of the cable going to the fixture to the switch's brass traveler terminals. Ground the switch in the same way as a middle-of-the-run switch *(page 52)*.

◆ At the fixture, connect the incoming white wire to the white fixture wire, join the two red wires in a wire cap, join the incoming black wire to the outgoing white (recoded black) wire with a wire cap, and connect the outgoing black wire to the black fixture wire with a cap. With a cap, fasten all the bare copper wires together, along with a green jumper wire to the ground screw of the box.

◆ At the second switch, fasten the black wire to the common terminal, and the red and white (recoded black) wires to the traveler terminals. Ground the switch as you would for a switch loop *(page 52)*.

INSTALLING RECESSED LIGHTING IN A WALLBOARD CEILING

1. Cutting the opening.
◆ Working on a stepladder with an electronic stud finder, locate the ceiling joists on each side of the proposed location of the fixture.
◆ Place the template provided by the manufacturer on the ceiling between two joists and trace it to mark the fixture opening.
◆ With the power to any circuits in the area turned off *(page 22)*, drill a small hole in the center of the circle. Then, bend a piece of coathanger wire to a 90-degree angle, insert one end through the hole, and rotate the wire to check for obstructions. If necessary, relocate the fixture.
◆ Cut the outline with a wallboard saw *(right)*.
◆ Unless your fixture is rated IC—for insulation contact—cut back any insulation at least 3 inches away from the opening.

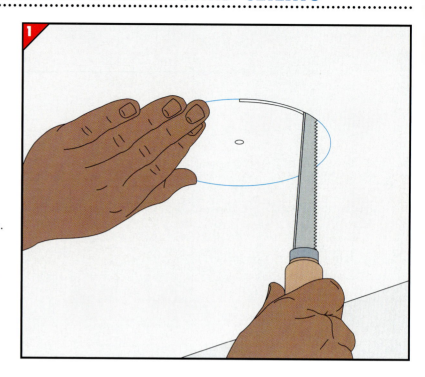

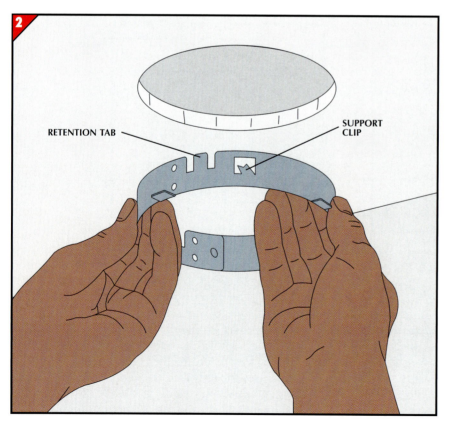

2. Installing the mounting frame.
◆ With a flat screwdriver, bend the support clips on the mounting frame inward at a 90-degree angle.
◆ Push the mounting frame into the opening *(left)*.
◆ Bend the three retention tabs outward so that they rest on top of the wallboard and support the mounting frame.

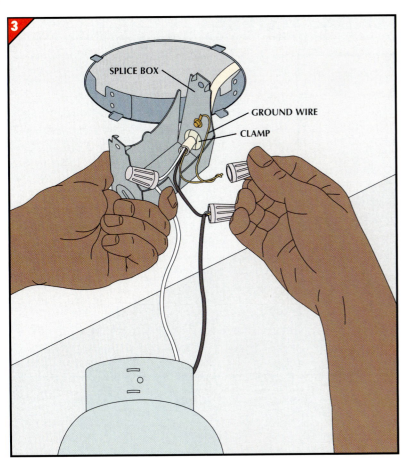

3. Connecting the wires.

◆ For a fixture controlled by a single-pole light switch *(page 52)*, fish two-conductor cable from the switch to the opening *(pages 48-49)*, then strip the insulation from the ends of the cable and wires *(pages 45-46)*.
◆ Detach the splice box from the fixture by removing the screws that hold it in place.
◆ Punch out a knockout from one end of the box, push the clamp provided with the switch kit into the hole from the outside, then pass the cable through the clamp.
◆ Rest the fixture on top of the ladder and, with the wire caps provided, connect the wires, white to white and black to black, and join the green or bare copper ground wire from the fixture to the ground wire of the cable *(left)*.
◆ Reattach the splice box to the fixture.

If the fixture is part of a three-way switch scheme *(pages 53-54)*—and is rated for this type of installation—fish two- or three-conductor cable to the splice box as appropriate for the lighting plan; then wire the fixture and the switches as shown on those pages.

4. Setting the fixture in place.

◆ Tilt the fixture to insert the splice box first *(right)*, then push it straight up into the mounting frame to secure it against the support clips.
◆ Wire the other end of the electrical cable to the switch as described on pages 52-54.

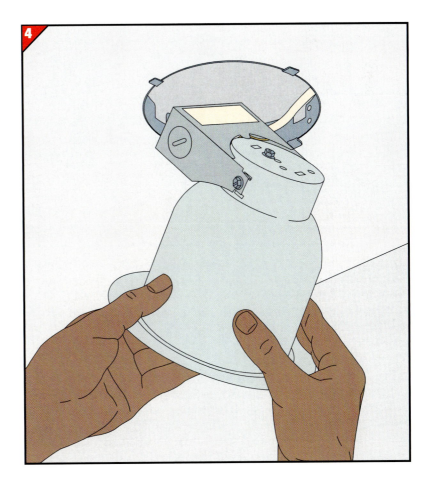

A BAR HANGER FOR A HEAVY CEILING FIXTURE

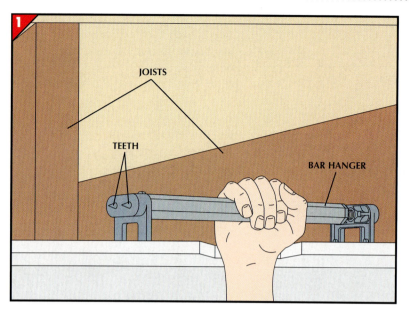

1. Positioning the hanger.
◆ Locate the joists near the proposed location of the fixture with an electronic stud finder and cut a hole for a ceiling box between two joists as you would for a recessed fixture *(page 56, Step 1)*.
◆ Slip the bar hanger into the hole and rest its feet on the top surface of the ceiling.
◆ Making sure the bar is perpendicular to the joists, turn it to extend the hanger until its ends reach the joists *(left)*.
◆ Fit an adjustable wrench over the bar and turn the wrench to force the teeth on the ends of the hanger into the joists.

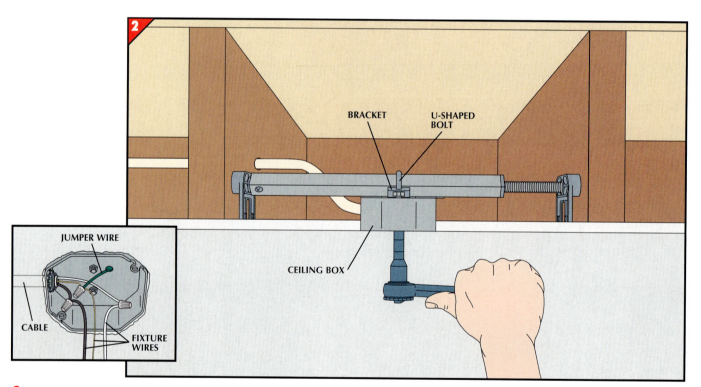

2. Securing the ceiling box.
◆ For a fixture controlled by a single-pole light switch *(page 52)*, fish two-conductor cable to the opening *(pages 48-49)*, remove one of the knockouts from the ceiling box, and secure the cable to the box with a clamp *(pages 49-50)*.
◆ Attach the box to the hanger bar using the hardware provided: Hang the U-shaped bolt over the bar, fit the bracket onto the bolt, then thread a nut over each end of the bolt. Tighten the nuts with a socket wrench, then fit the ceiling box and the support plate over the ends of the bolt and fasten them in place with the second set of nuts *(above)*.
◆ Strip the insulation off the cable and its wires *(pages 45-46)*, then connect the wires as shown in the inset: With wire caps, join the fixture wires to the cable wires—black to black and white to white. Strip off $\frac{1}{4}$ inch of insulation from both ends of a green jumper wire, then join the bare copper wires of the cable and fixture to the jumper with a wire cap *(page 46)*. Fasten the other end of the jumper to the ground screw in the box.
◆ Wire the other end of the cable to the switch as described on page 52.

If the fixture is part of a three-way switch scheme *(pages 53-55)*, run two- or three-conductor cable to the box and clamp it in place, then wire the fixture and switches as shown on those pages.

Putting In a Subpanel

Once you have run new branch circuits from outlets to the subpanel location, you can install the subpanel and run a feeder cable from it to the service panel.

Mounting the Box: If you are attaching the subpanel to a masonry surface, the easiest technique is to mount it on a plywood base *(pages 60-61)*. Where you will be flush-mounting it in wallboard, cut the hole in the wall so that the mounting side of the panel—the side without the knockouts—will be positioned against a stud. Once you have run the cables through the knockouts *(page 60, Step 3)*, fasten the box to the stud with 1-inch roundhead wood screws.

Hooking Up the Wires: A typical subpanel is fed with 240 volts from the main service panel by 6-gauge, 60-amp SER feeder cable, and contains breaker positions for anywhere from two to six branch circuits. To ground the cables in the subpanel box, buy a ground bus bar *(below)* that is appropriate for the model of subpanel you are installing.

When the new branch circuits supply only 120-volt service, buy single-pole circuit breakers for the panel *(page 61)*. If you are putting in an outlet for an electric range *(page 51)*, its three-conductor SER cable, which supplies 240 volts, will need a double-pole breaker—and a subpanel big enough to accommodate it. Ensure that each breaker is of the correct amperage for the type of circuit *(page 45, box)*. If there is an existing range receptacle that will no longer be used because the appliance is being relocated, have an electrician disconnect the existing cable at the service panel and remove the receptacle.

The feeder and the branch-circuit cables are run through knockout holes in the sides of the subpanel and secured there with special cable clamps. Though they serve the same purpose as the clamps in an outlet box *(page 50)*, they must be installed in the knockout holes before the cable is fed into the box.

When the new panel and circuits are in place, have an electrician hook the feeder cable to the service panel.

 TOOLS
Electric drill
Screwdriver
Carpenter's level
Hammer
Nail set
Cable ripper
Long-nose pliers
Lineman's pliers
Tin snips
Multipurpose tool

 MATERIALS
Subpanel box
Ground bus bar
Feeder cable
Cable clamps
Circuit breakers
Plywood ($\frac{3}{4}$")
Masonry screws and anchors
Roundhead wood screws ($\frac{1}{2}$")
Cable staples

 SAFETY TIPS
Goggles protect your eyes when you are operating a power tool.

WIRING THE BOX

1. Mounting the ground bus bar.
◆ Hold the bar where it will not interfere with the knockouts you will use, and align its mounting holes over two pre-tapped holes in the back of the box. If the panel has no pre-tapped holes, make them with a drill *(right)*.
◆ Fasten the bar in place with the screws provided.

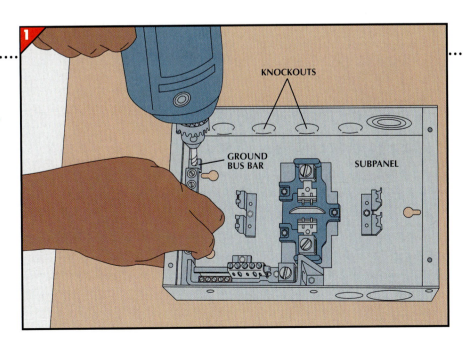

2. Hanging the box.

◆ For a surface-mounted box, cut a $\frac{3}{4}$-inch plywood base large enough to extend a few inches on all sides of the box.
◆ Screw the base to the wall at the subpanel location, drilling holes for masonry anchors first to fasten to a wall made of concrete blocks or concrete.
◆ With a helper holding the box centered on the base, mark the location of the top screw hole.
◆ Remove the box and drive a $\frac{1}{2}$-inch roundhead wood screw partially into the base.
◆ Slip the box onto the screw and drop the box down so the screw is in the narrow part of the opening. Level the box and tighten the screw, then drive the bottom screws into the narrow slots *(right)*.

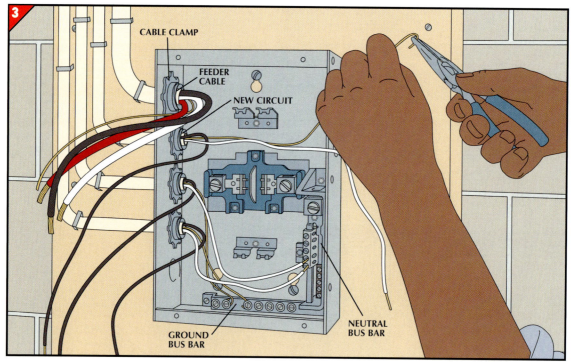

3. Connecting the circuit cables.

◆ With a hammer and nail set, remove the appropriate number of knockouts from one side of the subpanel box.
◆ Insert the feeder and circuit cables into the box through separate knockouts. Secure them to the box with cable clamps and to the base with cable staples. Strip the sheathing from the cables and remove the insulation from the individual wires *(pages 45-46)*.
◆ Working on one circuit at a time, form a hook in the stripped end of each bare copper ground wire with long-nose pliers *(above)* and connect the wire to a terminal of the ground bus bar.
◆ Connect each white neutral wire to a terminal of the neutral bus bar.

4. Wiring the circuit breakers.

◆ For 120-volt circuits, push the black lead of each cable into the terminal at the bottom front of a single-pole breaker of the proper amperage *(right)*, then tighten the setscrew.

◆ Slip the breaker over its guide hook in the panel box and snap the breaker down to lock it in place.

◆ Wire a 240-volt branch circuit in the same way, using a double-pole breaker of the correct amperage and inserting both the black and red leads into its terminals.

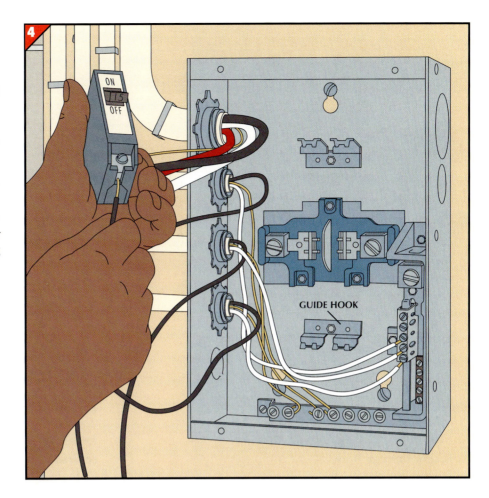

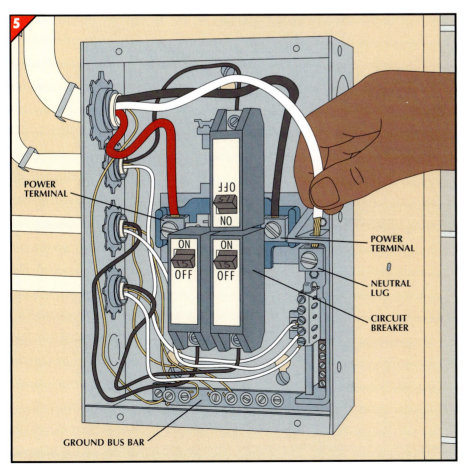

5. Connecting the feeder cable.

◆ In the subpanel box, attach the feeder cable's bare copper ground wire to the ground bus bar as you did the circuit ground wires in Step 3.

◆ Insert the stripped end of the red conductor into one of the subpanel power terminals and tighten the setscrew, then fasten the black conductor to the other power terminal in the same way.

◆ Attach the white feeder wire to the neutral lug at one end of the neutral bus bar *(left)* and tighten the setscrew.

◆ Have a licensed electrician hook up the feeder cable to the main panel.

Windows, Floors, and Walls

A few special touches can make a drab, stuffy kitchen bright and comfortable. Adding a window or putting in a larger unit can bring light to the space and provide a view of the outdoors, while a range hood can expel cooking heat and odors. For a complete rejuvenation, you can lay a ceramic-tile floor with a custom design, and install new wallboard and molding.

Opening a Wall For a New Window 64
Cutting Through Siding
Breaking Through Brick

Adding a Counter-Level Window 68
Framing the Opening
Setting a Vinyl Unit in Place

Creating a Wall of Natural Light 72
Putting in the Glass

Installing a Range Hood 75

Laying a Floor of Ceramic Tiles 78

Restoring Interior Walls 82
Techniques for Hanging Wallboard
Covering Screws and Corner Bead
Taping Joints
Dealing With Inside Corners
Concealing Seams

Finishing With Trim Molding 90
Applying Vinyl Wall Base
Installing Wooden Baseboards
Coping Contoured Molding

Laying a mortar bed for ceramic tiles →

Opening a Wall for a New Window

Adding a window to an exterior wall in the kitchen can brighten the room and make it seem more spacious. A window can also provide a source of fresh air.

Positioning the Opening: To determine the dimensions of the opening, buy the window first and size the opening to fit it. For a brick wall, choose a size that will enable you to place the opening along mortar joints as much as possible. If a new unit will match an existing window nearby, however, plan the size and position of the opening so that the two windows will align. Where plumbing or electrical lines are present, you will need to move them *(pages 36-39 and pages 48-52)* or choose a new site for the window.

Special Situations: Consult a professional if you plan an opening wider than 40 inches in a brick-veneer wall or in any bearing wall. Even a smaller opening in a bearing wall can cause sags or cracks during construction; avoid such problems with a temporary support wall built about 2 feet inside the house *(page 30, Step 2)*.

Making the Opening: For an exterior wall that is covered in wood, aluminum, vinyl, or stucco, use the method described below to cut away the siding. With a brick-veneer wall, you will need to cut a channel and install a steel lintel—available precut from a steel supplier *(page 66)*—before you remove the bricks from the opening.

 Before cutting into a wall, check for the presence of lead and asbestos (page 27), and turn off power to any circuits inside the wall.

 TOOLS
Straightedge
Electric drill
Electronic stud finder
Pry bar
Circular saw
Handsaw
Maul
Cold chisel
Screwdriver
Trowel
Stapler

 MATERIALS
Drop cloths
Angle irons ($1\frac{1}{2}$" x $1\frac{1}{2}$")
Wood screws (2" No. 10)
Steel lintel
Mortar mix
Bricks
Polyethylene sheeting (18 mil)
Plastic tubing ($\frac{3}{8}$")

 SAFETY TIPS
Wear a dust mask and goggles to cut siding. For demolishing a brick wall, add a hard hat, work gloves, a long-sleeved shirt, and sturdy shoes.

CUTTING THROUGH SIDING

Making the opening.
◆ Working from inside, mark the outline and remove the wallboard *(page 27, Step 1)* from floor to ceiling between the first studs beyond each side of the planned opening, leaving the studs in place; then pull out the insulation.
◆ Outline the rough opening on the sheathing and drill a hole through the sheathing and siding at each corner of the opening, then, from outside, draw a line connecting the holes using a straightedge.
◆ Fit a circular saw with a blade appropriate for the wall material—for stucco, a masonry blade or an old wood-cutting blade; for aluminum, a special abrasive blade; a plywood blade installed backwards for vinyl. Adjust the cutting depth to the thickness of the siding and the sheathing.
◆ Saw along the marked lines *(right)*, completing the cuts at the corners with a handsaw.
◆ Complete the interior opening, then install the window *(pages 68-71)*.

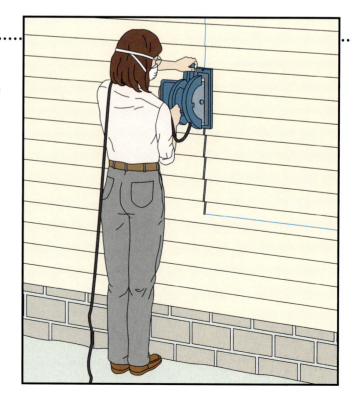

BREAKING THROUGH BRICK

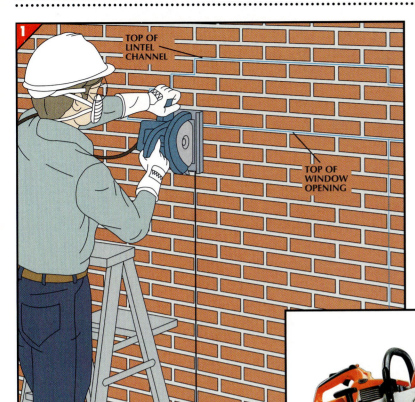

1. Scoring the opening.
- Mark the outline of the window opening as for a wall covered with siding *(opposite)*, but measure from the same reference point on both the interior and exterior walls rather than drilling guide holes.
- Four brick courses above the top of the window opening, draw a line representing the top of the lintel channel, then mark the channel sides in a stepped pattern so the top is the same width as the opening and the bottom is $1\frac{1}{2}$ bricks wider, forming a shoulder for the lintel *(page 66, Step 4)*.
- At the bottom of the window opening, outline a sill *(page 67, Step 7)*.
- Outfit a circular saw with a masonry blade set to cut $\frac{1}{2}$ inch deep, start the saw, and gradually work the blade into the wall along one side of the opening. A gas-powered masonry saw *(photograph)*, which can be rented, is specifically suited to cutting brick.
- Move the saw slowly along the line *(left)*, stopping frequently to let the blade cool.
- Score the opposite side, then the top and bottom of the opening, in the same way.

2. Cutting the lintel channel.
- With a cold chisel and maul, chip through the mortar joints at an upper corner of the lintel channel. Take out two bricks from the top course of the channel and three bricks from the next two courses.
- Fasten a $1\frac{1}{2}$- by $1\frac{1}{2}$-inch angle iron to each stud behind the sheathing—here covered with building paper—with 2-inch No. 10 wood screws, positioning the upper flange of the angle iron flat against the brick above it.
- Continue chipping at the mortar in the same way *(right)*, removing three bricks at a time from each of the top three courses, and attaching angle irons to the studs, until you reach the opposite edge of the channel.
- Take out the bottom course of bricks from the lintel channel.

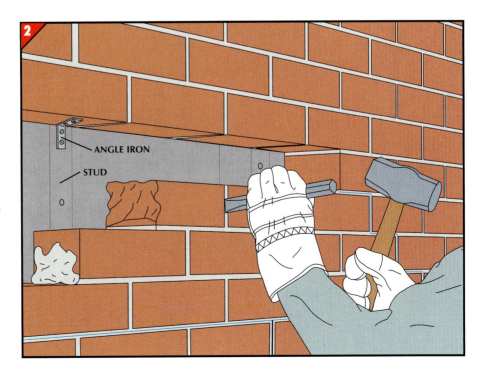

3. Completing the opening.
◆ Working from top to bottom and from the center to each side, take out the rest of the bricks from the opening, chipping mortar out of the joints to loosen them *(right)*. Try to leave some bricks whole—you will need them to fill the space above the lintel and to build the sill.
◆ To break off half bricks cleanly at the sides of the opening, wedge the cold chisel—or a special broad-bladed chisel called a brick set—into the saw cut and rap it sharply with the maul.

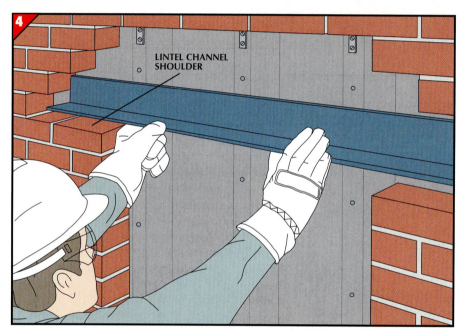

4. Setting the lintel.
◆ Chip away bits of mortar from the top of the bricks that form the shoulders of the lintel channel.
◆ Lift the lintel into its channel *(left)*, setting the horizontal flange on the shoulders and the vertical flange against the sheathing.

5. Adding plastic flashing.
◆ Cut a slit in the building paper just above the lintel with a utility knife.
◆ Slip a length of 18-mil plastic under the bottom of the building paper to serve as flashing. Drive staples through the building paper and flashing into the studs between the lintel and the angle irons *(right)*.
◆ Lap the flashing completely over the lintel, then trim it to leave $\frac{1}{2}$ inch of the horizontal lintel flange exposed.
◆ Lay plastic flashing over the bricks at the bottom of the window opening, draping it along the outside of the sheathing.

6. Filling in the channel.

◆ Clean off old mortar from bricks that you reuse, and dampen—not soak—them with water so they do not draw moisture from fresh mortar.
◆ Working from one end of the lintel to the other, apply mortar to the end of a brick and slide it onto the lintel, butting it against its neighbor. Every third vertical joint, place a piece of $\frac{3}{8}$-inch plastic tubing at the base of the bricks to form a weep hole for escaping moisture *(right)*.
◆ Lay a mortar bed for the next course of bricks and continue, adjusting the size of joints between bricks as necessary to align them with their respective courses in the wall.

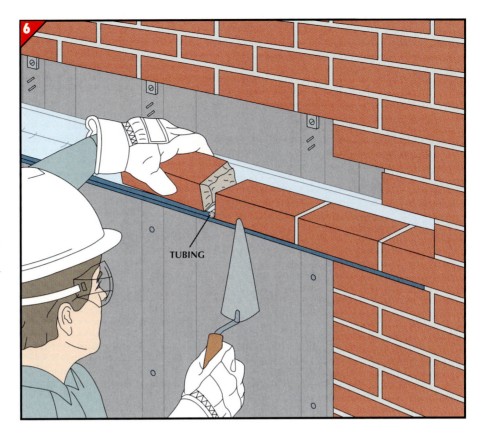

7. Making a masonry sill.

Finish the exterior sill to match those of the other windows of your house.
◆ For a sill of rowlock bricks—a row of bricks on edge—apply mortar and lay the course at the bottom of the opening *(left)*. Make the back of the mortar bed about $\frac{1}{2}$ inch thicker than the front so the bricks will slope to shed water. Adjust the thickness of the bed to bring the top of the bricks to the level of the bottom of the window.
◆ Leave a $\frac{3}{8}$-inch gap between the bricks for mortar, but adjust the joints so you finish the course with a whole brick. Leave weep holes as in Step 6.
◆ Cut away the wall sheathing, then install the window *(pages 68-71)*.

For a precast concrete sill, order one 8 inches longer than the width of the opening, removing bricks at the edges to make a shoulder on each side. Lay the sill on a bed of mortar so it sits flush with the bottom of the opening, its outside edge extending $\frac{1}{2}$ inch from the face of the wall.

Adding a Counter-Level Window

For a window that is over a kitchen counter, a casement-style unit *(below)* is a wise choice; with its crank mechanism, it can be opened and closed with much greater ease than the double-hung type. Since the sashes can open to the right or left, determine the direction in which you want them to swing before buying a window.

Choosing a Type: Windows are available in several materials. Those made of wood have good insulation properties, but they must be painted periodically to prevent rot. Vinyl models are nearly maintenance-free, but do not keep out temperature extremes as well as wood. Windows built of vinyl- or aluminum-clad wood combine energy efficiency with durability.

Choose a model whose glass is also well insulated—with two or three panes instead of one, or with the space between panes filled with argon gas. Special low-emissive (low-e) glass is especially effective at keeping heat in or out.

There are several methods for finishing the exterior—when you order the window, discuss your plans with the dealer to determine the best one for your installation.

Framing the Opening: Before you can install the window, you will need to build a rough frame with a strong header *(opposite)* to support the wall above the opening and to provide a surface to which the window can be mounted.

  TOOLS

Circular saw
Pry bar
Hammer
Tin snips
Carpenter's level
Screwdriver
Utility knife
Electronic stud finder
Caulking gun

 **MATERIALS**

2 x 4s
Lumber for header
Lumber for jamb extensions
Plywood ($\frac{1}{2}$")
Casing stock
Shims
Common nails ($2\frac{1}{2}$", $3\frac{1}{2}$")
Finishing nails ($1\frac{1}{2}$", 2")
Wood screws ($1\frac{1}{4}$")
Prefabricated drip cap
Fiberglass insulation
Wallboard repair materials
Caulk

  SAFETY TIPS

Goggles protect your eyes when you are nailing or using a power tool. Put on gloves, long sleeves, goggles, and a dust mask when handling fiberglass insulation.

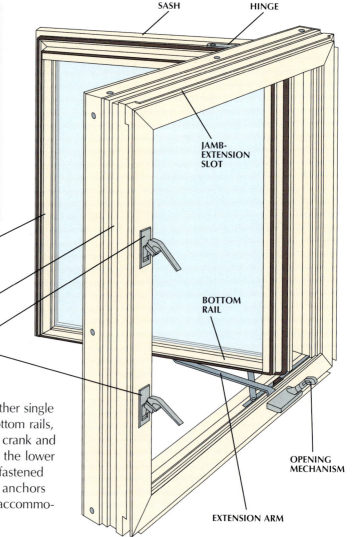

A casement window.
On casement windows, the sashes—whether single or double—are hinged to the top and bottom rails, and open outward by means of a geared crank and an extension arm that slides in a track on the lower rail. The vinyl-clad model shown here is fastened to the rough framing with special metal anchors *(page 71, Step 2)*. Slots around the sash accommodate jamb extensions *(page 71, Step 3)*.

A STURDY HEADER

Window headers *(right)* can be made from two lengths of lumber sandwiched around a piece of plywood *(page 70)*. The size of the lumber depends on several factors, including the width of the opening and how much weight the wall bears *(page 26)*. Consult a lumber dealer or local building codes to determine what size is right for your opening.

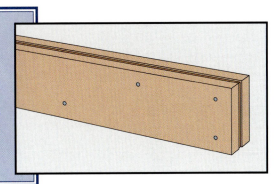

FRAMING THE OPENING

1. Removing studs.
◆ With a circular saw, make an angled cut through the middle of each stud in the wall opening.
◆ Lever the studs away from the remaining exterior sheathing with a pry bar, taking care not to tear the sheathing near the edges of the opening.
◆ Pull the studs away from the top plate and the soleplate *(left)*.

2. Constructing the frame.
◆ For each side of the opening, cut 2-by-4 studs: a king stud that fits from the soleplate to the top plate and a jack stud that runs from the soleplate to the top of the opening. (An existing stud $1\frac{1}{2}$ inches from the edge of the opening can serve as a king stud.)
◆ Plumb the studs with a carpenter's level, aligning the jack studs along the inside edges of the opening, then toenail the studs to the top plate and soleplate with $3\frac{1}{2}$-inch common nails, and nail them to each other with $2\frac{1}{2}$-inch nails *(right)*.

3. Putting in the header.
◆ Cut two header boards *(page 69)* to fit horizontally between the king studs, then trim a piece of $\frac{1}{2}$-inch plywood to fit between the boards so the header is the proper thickness. Nail the pieces together with $3\frac{1}{2}$ inch nails, staggering them along the length of the lumber.
◆ Set the header on edge on the jack studs and fasten it in place by driving two $3\frac{1}{2}$-inch nails through the king studs into each end of the header *(above)*.

4. Finishing the rough frame.
◆ Measure between the header and the top plate, then cut a 2-by-4 cripple stud to this length for every location where a regular stud was removed. Toenail the cripple studs in place with $2\frac{1}{2}$-inch nails.
◆ To make the rough sill, cut a 2-by-4 to fit between the jack studs. Align its top with the bottom of the opening and toenail it to the jack studs with $2\frac{1}{2}$-inch nails.
◆ Cut a cripple stud to fit between the soleplate and the sill at each point where a regular stud was removed, as well as against the jack stud on each side of the opening.
◆ Drive a $3\frac{1}{2}$-inch nail through the sill into the top of each cripple stud *(right)*, then toenail the bottom of each stud to the soleplate with $2\frac{1}{2}$-inch nails.

SETTING A VINYL UNIT IN PLACE

1. Adding drip cap.
For a wall with siding, you will need to install a drip cap. It is not required on a brick-veneer wall because the window will be recessed into the brick. Buy a prefabricated drip cap the same width and depth as the window's top brickmold, or exterior trim.
◆ With tin snips, cut the cap to the length and height of the brickmold.
◆ Insert the drip cap between the building paper and the sheathing *(right)*.

2. Fastening the window.
◆ Snap the anchors *(photograph)* that come with the window into the mounting grooves in the frame, placing two per side, as specified by the window manufacturer.
◆ Have a helper tilt the window into the opening and rest the outer edge securely on the rough sill.
◆ While your helper holds the window, insert shims between the window and the rough frame at the anchor positions *(left)*.
◆ With a carpenter's level, check that the unit is level and plumb, adjusting the shims as necessary, then screw the anchors to the frame through the shims with $1\frac{1}{4}$-inch No. 8 wood screws. With a utility knife, score the shims flush with the rough frame, then break them off.
◆ Fill the spaces between the window and the rough frame with fiberglass insulation, avoiding compacting it.

3. Extending the jambs.
To extend the jamb of the window flush with the face of the finished wall, wood strips are inserted into the jamb-extension slots around the perimeter of the window.
◆ To calculate the width of the strips, measure the distance from the bottom of the jamb-extension slot to the surface of the rough frame and add the wallboard thickness.
◆ From lumber the thickness of the jamb-extension slot, cut a strip of the calculated width to the length of the top slot, then push it into the slot *(right)*. Cut and insert strips for the other slots in the same way.

Patch the wallboard around the opening *(pages 82-89)*, add casing *(page 74, Steps 5-6)*, and attach the handle to the opening mechanism. Finish the exterior *(page 68)*, and seal gaps with exterior caulk.

Creating a Wall of Natural Light

Tall windows can brighten a kitchen or provide a pleasant view of a garden or patio. Where there is an existing window, you can often replace it with a taller one; but for a wood-frame wall with no windows, you can still accomplish the job without major structural changes.

Planning the Job: To add a window where there is none, simply remove narrow sections of wall between studs and install custom-made units. As many as three adjoining spaces between studs can be opened in this way without affecting the structural integrity of the wall. Whenever possible, avoid a location that requires plumbing, wiring, or heating ducts to be rerouted. Before you order the windows, cut small holes near the studs within the proposed opening to determine the exact distance between them.

Choosing Windows: Order the windows $\frac{1}{2}$ inch shorter than the height of the proposed rough opening and $\frac{1}{2}$ inch narrower than the distance between studs, and specify the wall thickness as well as the overall dimensions so the manufacturer can provide jambs of the proper depth. Plate-glass windows will do the job, but units that have two layers of glass with an air space between are more energy efficient. Make sure the sills are sloped to allow rainwater to run off, and order separate brickmold—the exterior trim—to finish the installation.

 Before cutting into walls, follow the precautions on page 27 regarding lead and asbestos.

 TOOLS

Electronic stud finder
Circular saw
Electric drill
Backsaw
Carpenter's level
Adjustable T-bevel
Manual or power miter saw
Nail set
Caulking gun

 **MATERIALS**

Window units and brickmold
1 x 4s, 2 x 4s
Shims
Trim stock ($\frac{1}{2}$")
Casing stock
Common nails ($3\frac{1}{2}$")
Assorted finishing nails
Prefabricated drip cap
Exterior caulk
Wood putty or spackling compound

 SAFETY TIPS

Wear goggles when you are driving nails or operating a power tool.

PUTTING IN THE GLASS

1. Preparing the opening.

◆ Locate studs and mark an opening of the desired height and width, with each side of the opening along the inner edge of a stud.
◆ Remove the wallboard *(page 27, Step 1)*—cutting only within the outline and leaving the studs intact—then move outdoors to complete the opening in the exterior wall *(pages 64-67)*.
◆ If the exterior wall is siding, mark a line outside the opening indicating the amount by which the brickmold will extend beyond the jambs at the top and sides. Set the depth of a circular saw blade to the thickness of the siding alone and make a cut along the line *(inset)*.
◆ Cut 2-by-4 headers to fit between the studs at the top of the opening and toenail them to the studs with $3\frac{1}{2}$-inch common nails, ensuring their bottom edges align with the cut in the wallboard.
◆ Trim 2-by-4 cripple studs $1\frac{1}{2}$ inches shorter than the distance between the bottom of the opening and the soleplate, then nail them to the sides of the full studs.
◆ For the rough sills, cut 2-by-4s to fit snugly between each pair of full studs and nail them to the cripple studs *(right)*.

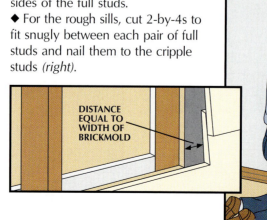

2. Adjusting the sills.
◆ A brick-veneered house needs no drip cap above the window, but for a house with siding, use tin snips to cut a section of prefabricated drip cap with a width equal to the thickness of the brickmold to fit along the top of the opening. Slit the building paper at the top of the opening and slide the drip cap between the building paper and the sheathing.
◆ On the interior of the opening, nail temporary 1-by-4 braces to the studs near the top and bottom of the opening.
◆ Tilt the center window into place against the braces. Mark the midpoint of the stud on each side of the window; if the sill horns extend beyond the midpoints, mark the excess *(left)*, remove the window, and trim it with a backsaw.
◆ Trim the excess horn from each sill in the same way so that when all the units are installed there is one continuous sill.
◆ Remove the temporary braces.

3. Fastening the frames.
◆ Set the center window back in place and, with a helper holding it on the outside, use a carpenter's level to plumb and level it indoors, wedging shims about every 12 inches between the side jambs and studs *(right)* as well as between the bottom jamb and sill.
◆ Secure the unit by driving 3-inch finishing nails through the side jambs and shims into the studs. Drive a single nail at the top into the center of the header and another one at the bottom into the center of the sill.
◆ Install the adjoining window units following the same procedure.
◆ Score the shims flush with the studs with a utility knife and snap off the excess.

4. Trimming the exterior.

◆ No brickmold is required for a brick-veneered house, but for a house with siding, cut a piece of brickmold to fit along the top of the windows, cutting the ends square for butt joints or mitering them as on the interior trim *(Step 5)*. Fasten the brickmold with galvanized 3-inch finishing nails.
◆ With an adjustable T-bevel, transfer the slope of the sill to the bottom edge of two side brickmold pieces *(left)*, then make the cuts with a miter saw. Cut the top of the pieces to fit against the top brickmold, then nail them in place.
◆ Cut $\frac{1}{2}$-inch-thick trim strips to cover the combined width of the stud and jambs framing each window unit, beveling the bottoms to fit the sill. Cut another piece to run across the front edge of the sill, then fasten the strips with $1\frac{1}{2}$-inch galvanized finishing nails.
◆ Caulk any gaps along the brickmold and sill.

5. Cutting the interior trim.

◆ Cut four lengths of casing, each one long enough to span one side of the opening and allow for a miter at each end—usually an extra 10 to 12 inches.
◆ Mark the distance between the two outer jambs on the inner edges of the top and bottom pieces, centering the measurement, then use a miter saw to cut each end at a 45-degree angle outward from the marks *(right)*.
◆ Cut side pieces in the same way, using an inside measurement equal to the distance between the inner edges of the top and bottom jambs.

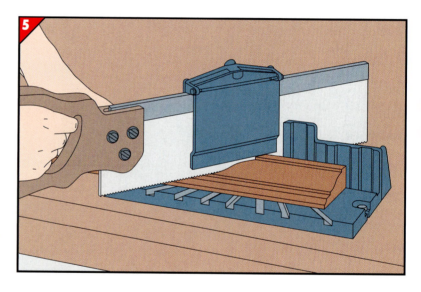

6. Fastening the trim pieces.

◆ Nail the casing in place around the windows at 6-inch intervals, driving $1\frac{1}{2}$-inch finishing nails through the narrow part and 2-inch nails through the wide part.
◆ Protecting the wall surface with a piece of cardboard, lock-nail each mitered corner with $1\frac{1}{2}$-inch nails, driving one vertically and one horizontally into the wide edges of the casing *(inset)*.
◆ Nail filler strips to the studs between the windows to bring them flush with the jambs, then cover them with trim.
◆ Sink all the nail heads with a nail set *(left)* and fill the holes with wood putty or, if painting the window units, with spackling compound.

Installing a Range Hood

Cooking vapors and odors, as well as airborne grease, can be eliminated from kitchen air by means of a range hood. The powerful fan in these units pulls air through a filter and expels it to the outdoors.

Planning the Installation: Range hoods are available in a variety of sizes and designs, and may be mounted under cabinets, on walls, or suspended from the ceiling. They are rated according to the number of cubic feet of air they move per minute (CFM), but this figure is affected by the length and configuration of the ductwork between the hood and the outdoors. Ideally, the vent duct should go straight out the wall behind the stove along the shortest route possible *(below)*. If there are obstructions in the wall such as pipes or wiring, you may be able to add elbows to route ducts through another area. In some instances, you may have to vent the hood through the roof. These arrangements reduce the system's efficiency, however, and require a hood with a more powerful fan. Before you buy a unit, plan the installation, then check the manufacturer's specifications to determine the CFM you need.

If the placement of the stove makes it difficult to access an outside wall, you can substitute a ductless range hood. Though efficient at filtering smoke and odors, these units cannot remove heat and moisture from the room.

Preparing the Cabinet: Range hoods are intended to be attached to a flat surface. If the cabinet you will be fastening it to has a recessed bottom, screw wood filler strips into the recess to bring it flush with the outer frame.

CAUTION *Before you cut into the wall, check for the presence of lead and asbestos (page 27).*

TOOLS

Hammer
Nail set
Screwdriver
Electric drill
Extension bit
Wallboard saw
Saber saw
Circular saw
Tin snips
Caulking gun
Wiring tools

MATERIALS

Wood strips ($\frac{1}{2}$")
Galvanized wood screws ($1\frac{1}{2}$" No. 8)
Sheet-metal screws ($\frac{1}{2}$" No. 8)
Caulk
Electrical cable
Cable clamp
Wire nuts

SAFETY TIPS

Wear goggles when operating power tools.

Venting through a wall.
The range hood shown here fastens to the underside of the cabinet over the stove; it typically comes with its fan and light fixture already wired and mounted. The vent duct is passed in through the outside wall and screwed to a transition bracket that joins it to the hood. The assembly features a wall cap with a damper that prevents air from flowing back in when the fan is not running.

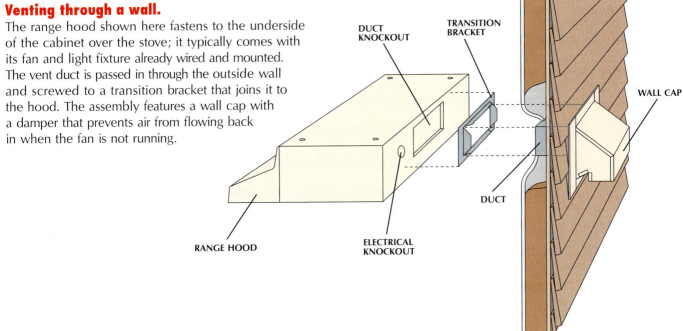

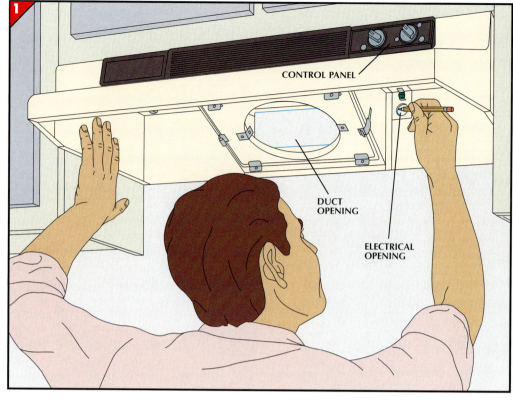

1. Positioning the hood.
◆ With a hammer and nail set, punch out the knockouts for the duct and electrical wires. Remove the fan from its mounting clips, unplug its electrical connection, then pull it from the unit.
◆ While a helper holds the hood in place—its front edge containing the control panel in line with the outer edge of the cabinet—trace the large end of the hood's keyhole-shaped mounting holes onto the cabinet bottom.
◆ Lower the hood and drive the supplied screws partway into the marked holes.
◆ Fasten the hood in place and outline the duct and electrical openings *(right)*. If the back of the hood does not fit snug against the wall, also draw a reference line along its back edge on the bottom of the cabinet.
◆ Turn off power to any circuits in the wall *(page 22)*, then fit an electric drill with an extension bit and bore a hole through the wall in each corner of the outlined duct opening to mark its position on the outer wall.
◆ Cut a hole through the wallboard at the marked duct and electrical openings with a keyhole saw.

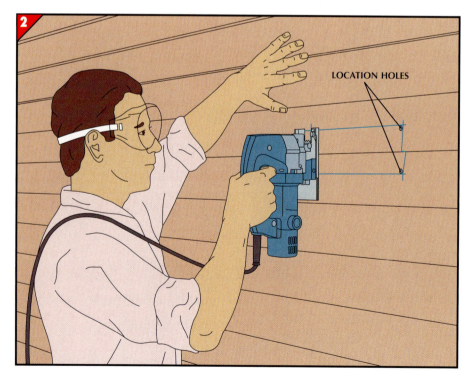

2. Cutting the exterior opening.
◆ On the outside wall, use a straightedge to connect the four location holes and mark the duct opening.
◆ With a saber saw, cut through the siding and sheathing along the marked lines *(left)*.

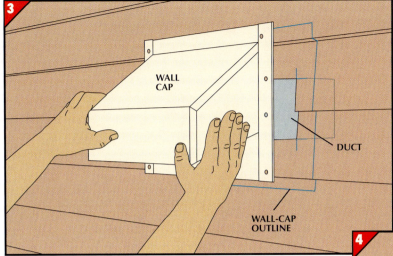

3. Preparing to mount the wall cap.
◆ Slide the duct through the opening in the wall. Position the wall-cap assembly against the siding and mark its outline, then remove it *(left)*.
◆ Set the blade of a circular saw to the depth of the siding only and cut along the marked line.
◆ Butt $\frac{1}{2}$- by 1-inch wood strips against the cut edges of the siding along all four sides of the opening and fasten them to the sheathing with galvanized $1\frac{1}{2}$-inch No. 8 wood screws.

4. Installing the duct assembly.
◆ Have a helper insert the duct assembly into the hole. For a hood that sits against the wall, draw a line around the duct flush with the interior wall; in the case of a hood that stops short of the wall, mark the duct even with the reference line you drew on the bottom of the cabinet *(Step 1)*.
◆ Remove the assembly and cut the duct along the mark with tin snips.
◆ Insert the tabs of the transition bracket into the duct and drill pilot holes for $\frac{1}{2}$-inch No. 8 sheet-metal screws through the duct and each side tab, then remove the bracket.
◆ From the outside, fasten the duct assembly to the wood strips around the hole with galvanized $1\frac{1}{2}$-inch No. 8 wood screws, then caulk around the flange *(right)*.
◆ Inside the house, screw the transition bracket to the duct, then apply the bracket's self-adhesive sealing strip to the face of the bracket.

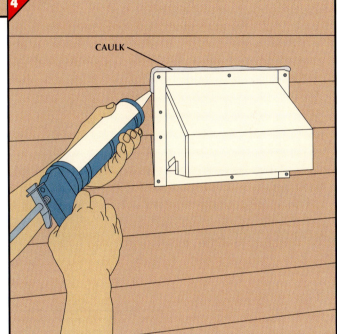

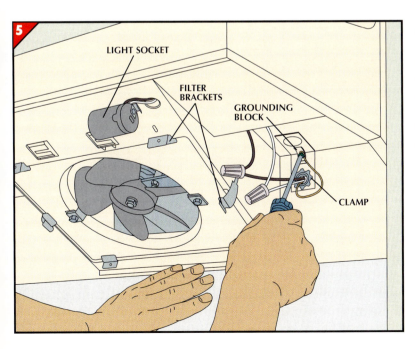

5. Completing the installation.
◆ Replace the fan in the hood and plug in its electrical connection.
◆ Run cable from the power source to the wire opening in the wall *(pages 48-49)*.
◆ With a helper holding the hood, feed the cable through its knockout hole and fasten it there with a cable clamp.
◆ Slide the hood along the mounting screws to butt it against the transition bracket, then tighten the screws.
◆ Connect the black wires with a wire cap *(page 46)*, then cap the white wires. Screw the cable's bare copper wire to the hood's grounding block *(left)*. Have an electrician wire the other end of the cable to the service panel.
◆ Screw a bulb into the light socket, then clip the filter into its brackets.

Laying a Floor of Ceramic Tiles

Attractive and durable, ceramic tiles are a good choice for a kitchen floor. A great variety of patterns can be achieved simply by combining tiles of different sizes and colors.

Selecting Materials: If you have removed old cabinetry, install the new units before you plan a design *(Chapter 4)*. Lay out the arrangement of tiles on graph paper *(below)* to determine how many tiles of each size and color you need, then add five to ten percent to allow for breakage. Take the plan with you when you purchase the materials.

Tile with an abrasive grain is best for a kitchen, since a smooth surface can become slippery when wet. Glazed tiles are impermeable to liquid, and therefore will not absorb stains; but some types—quarry tile, for example—require an application of a protective sealant.

For setting tiles, buy a thin-set mortar modified with a latex or polymer additive for water resistance. Choose a modified Portland-cement grout to fill joints and a grout sealant to protect it from staining. Make sure the products are appropriate for the type of tile you have selected.

Preparing for the Job: Before you begin, check that the floor is smooth and stable. If you are laying tile directly on a subfloor, repair or replace it if necessary *(page 33)*, then build it up to a thickness of $1\frac{1}{4}$ inches to prevent it from flexing and cracking the tiles. You can set tile over existing ceramic or vinyl flooring, as long as the flooring is in good repair and well bonded, but do not lay tiles on a hardwood floor. Remove any baseboards and shoe molding, then lay out a dry run *(opposite)* to ensure that the design you have planned will fit.

 TOOLS

Hammer
Tape measure
Chalk lines
Mason's trowel
Notched trowel
Mallet
Carpenter's level
Tile cutter
Grout float
Sponge

 **MATERIALS**

Graph paper
Ceramic tiles
Thin-set mortar
2 x 4
Tile spacers
Grout
Grout sealant

 SAFETY TIPS

Wear rubber gloves when spreading mortar and grout. Knee pads will make your work more comfortable.

1. Planning on paper.

◆ On graph paper, mark off the room's shape and size, letting each square represent the size of the smallest tile you will be using.
◆ Plot a design, filling in the squares with different colors to represent the different sizes and colors of tile. Darken the outline of large tiles that are represented by more than one small square.

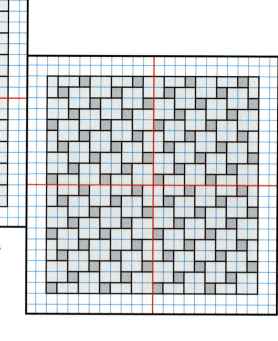

◆ Divide the pattern into equal quadrants. In some layouts, such as a square pattern, tiles will line up along the quadrant lines *(above)*; in others, such as a scattered design, some tiles will overlap adjoining quadrants *(right)*.
◆ Count the number of each type of tile you will need.

2. Guidelines for a dry run.

◆ Tap a nail into the subfloor at the midpoint of each wall, right next to the wall or at the cabinet along it. String chalk lines between the nails to divide the floor into equal quadrants.

◆ To check that the strings are perpendicular, mark off 3 feet along one line, starting where the two strings intersect, and 4 feet along the other line. Measure between the two marked points *(left)*. If the diagonal distance is exactly 5 feet, the lines are square; otherwise, reposition the nails and repeat the test.

3. Making the dry run.

◆ Following the pattern established in Step 1, place a row of tiles without mortar along each of the guidelines defining one quadrant *(right)*. For a scattered pattern, such as the one shown, make sure that tiles straddling the line are centered directly over it.

◆ Where both tile rows end more than half a tile width from the wall, lift the tiles and snap both chalk lines. If the space at the end of either row is less than half a tile width, move the chalk line perpendicular to that row to either side by exactly one half the width of a tile before snapping the chalk line.

4. Laying the mortar bed.

◆ With a mason's trowel, mix thin-set mortar according to the manufacturer's directions. Add more of the dry ingredients if the mortar is soupy and does not form ridges. If the mortar is dry and crumbly, add water.
◆ At the intersection of the chalk lines, spread a low mound of mortar with a notched trowel. Holding the trowel almost vertical, pull its toothed side through the mortar, leaving shallow grooves *(left)*.
◆ Sprinkle a few drops of water on the back of a tile; if the drops are absorbed easily, sponge water onto the back of each tile before setting it.
◆ Place the tile on the mortar bed, pressing it down firmly. Twist the tile several times to ensure good contact with the mortar *(inset)*.
◆ Lift the tile to inspect the bond created. If you see a pattern of ridges or if the bottom of the tile is less than 90 percent covered with mortar, use a trowel with larger notches to make a new bed, then relay the tile.

◆ With the handle of the mason's trowel, tap the tile to align it with the chalked lines.
◆ Place a carpenter's level on the tile diagonally and along two adjacent sides to check for level. Tap down high sides with a mallet and a 2-by-4 wrapped in cloth.

5. Filling in the field.

◆ Follow your pattern to set tiles along each of the chalk lines defining the edge of one quadrant. With a scattered pattern, some tiles will straddle the lines, while for a square pattern, simply lay the tiles flush to the line *(inset)*. Unless the tiles are made with spacing lugs along their bottom edges, set rubber or plastic tile spacers between them as you go.
◆ Check the row of tiles for level with a carpenter's level placed on a straight 2-by-4, tapping down any high tiles as described in Step 4.
◆ Fill in each quadrant in turn, respecting the pattern you have set out in your plan. Measure out from the chalk lines frequently and enlarge the spacing between tiles as needed to keep tiles aligned and the rows even.
◆ After every few tiles, check the tiles for level *(right)* and tap down any high ones.

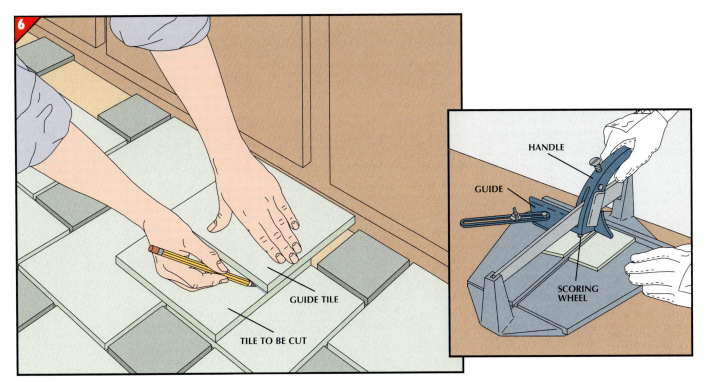

6. Cutting border tiles.

◆ Wherever the pattern does not reach all the way to the wall, place two loose tiles squarely on top of the last whole tile at the end of a row. Slide the upper of the two tiles across the gap until it touches the wall.
◆ With the top tile as a guide, mark the bottom tile *(above)*.

◆ Using a rented tile cutter, set the guide to position the tile's marked cutting line under the scoring wheel. Pull the scoring wheel across the tile, then press down on the handle to snap the tile *(inset)*.
◆ Lay the cut tiles in the same manner as the tiles in the field.

7. Spreading grout.

◆ Let the tile set overnight, then remove tile spacers if they were used.
◆ Mix grout following the package directions and pour approximately 1 cup of grout onto the tiles.
◆ Working on a section of tile 5 feet square, hold a grout float at a 45-degree angle to the floor and sweep it diagonally across the joints several times to force the grout between the tiles *(right)*.
◆ Turn the float on its edge and compact each joint so the grout is slightly below the surface of the tiles.
◆ Drag a clean float over the floor to remove any excess grout, then follow with a damp sponge. If the sponge pulls grout from between tiles, let the grout dry longer before continuing.
◆ Follow the same technique to grout the rest of the floor section-by-section. When all sections have set for 10 to 15 minutes, wipe the tile with a damp cloth to remove any haze.
◆ Misting the grout periodically, let it cure for several days until it becomes a uniform light color.
◆ For unglazed tile, apply sealant to the entire floor. Otherwise, brush grout sealant onto the joints only. Allow the sealant to dry before walking on the floor.

Restoring Interior Walls

When a time-worn kitchen undergoes a major renovation, it may be necessary to remove old, damaged wall materials and replace them with new wallboard. And if an addition has been built to accommodate a new, larger kitchen, you can cut costs by finishing the walls yourself. Where bearing or nonbearing walls have been removed *(pages 26-32)*, plumbing lines extended *(pages 36-39)*, or openings cut for windows *(pages 64-74)*, you can also use the techniques on these pages to patch gaps left behind. Before you begin, complete planned electrical modifications *(pages 44-61)* and make sure exterior walls are properly insulated.

Installing Panels: For greatest holding power, use wallboard adhesive and screws to fasten the sheets in place. Hang any ceiling panels first, then cover the walls, always beginning in a corner. Except on narrow walls, install the panels horizontally to minimize the number of joints. Use standard $\frac{1}{2}$-inch-thick panels measuring 4 by 8 feet, unless the ceiling is higher than 8 feet; in this case, you can sometimes install $4\frac{1}{2}$-foot-wide sheets on the walls to avoid the need for filler strips at the bottom. Trim panels so joints fall at the center of joists or studs and end-to-end joints are offset by at least one joist or stud in adjacent rows.

Joints and Screwheads: After the wallboard is in place, protect outside corners with corner bead *(page 85)* and conceal the joints and screwheads to make a smooth surface for painting *(pages 86-89)*.

 TOOLS

Wallboard saw
Chalk line
Caulking gun
Wallboard T-square
Utility knife
Electric drill
Clutch-driven screwdriver bit
Pry bar
Tin snips
Taping knives (5", 8", 10")

 **MATERIALS**

Wallboard panels ($\frac{1}{2}$")
Wallboard screws ($1\frac{1}{2}$")
Wallboard adhesive
Corner bead
Joint compound
Paper joint tape
Sandpaper (120-grit)

SAFETY TIPS

Wear goggles when operating power tools and applying joint compound overhead. Put on a dust mask to sand.

TECHNIQUES FOR HANGING WALLBOARD

Cutting panels.
To trim a panel so the ends fall at the center of a joist or stud, or to obtain a piece smaller than 4 by 8 feet, cut it to fit.
◆ Measure and mark the wallboard, then place a wallboard T-square at the mark and score the paper with a utility knife *(right)*.
◆ Grasp the edge of the panel on both sides of the cut and snap the short section away from you, breaking the wallboard along the cut.
◆ Cock the short section back slightly, then reach behind the panel with the knife and make a foot-long slit in the paper along the bend.
◆ Snap the short section forward to break it off.

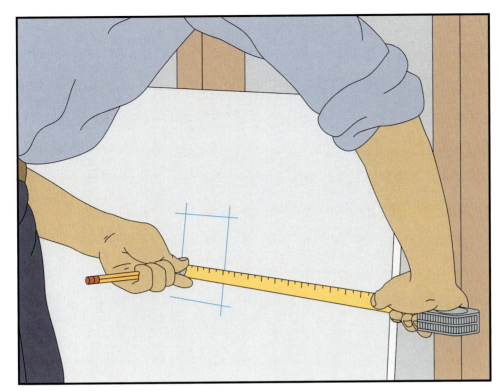

Making openings.
◆ To mark a panel for an opening such as an electrical box, measure from the point on the wall where the edge of the sheet will rest to the near and far sides of the box.

◆ Similarly, measure from the point where the top or bottom of the panel will fall to the top and bottom of the box.
◆ Transfer these measurements to the wallboard (above), then cut the opening with a wallboard or keyhole saw.

Applying adhesive.
Run a $\frac{3}{8}$-inch-thick bead of wallboard adhesive along the center of each ceiling joist or wall stud that the wallboard will cover (right), starting and stopping about 6 inches from where the edges will fall to prevent adhesive from oozing out between the sheets.

Fastening sheets to the ceiling.
◆ Fit an electric drill with a clutch-driven screwdriver bit *(photograph)*—also called a dimpler—which automatically stops screws at the correct depth.
◆ With a helper or two, lift the panel into place against the adhesive-coated ceiling joists.
◆ Drive a $1\frac{1}{2}$-inch wallboard screw into each joist at the center of the sheet *(left)*.
◆ Fasten the sides of the panel to each joist, driving screws 1 inch from the edges.
◆ At the ends of the panel, $\frac{1}{2}$ inch from the edge, drive screws into the joists every 16 inches.
◆ Hang the rest of the panels in the same manner, staggering the end joints in adjacent rows by at least one joist.

Adding filler strips.
When a whole panel does not reach to the edge of the ceiling, you can patch the gap with a filler strip cut from the sides of a sheet so that the tapered edges of the wallboard meet at the joint. Where the ceiling joists run perpendicular to the filler, cut a narrow piece and fasten it to the joists *(above)*. If the joists run parallel to the strip, plan the installation so that the filler will span at least two joists.

Horizontal wall panels.

◆ Mark the centers of studs on the ceiling and floor, and trim the first panel to end at the center of a stud *(page 82)*.
◆ Apply adhesive to the studs *(page 83, bottom)* and, with a helper, lift the panel into place against the ceiling *(above)*.
◆ With a dimpler *(opposite)* on the drill, drive screws into each stud 1 inch from the bottom, across the middle, and 1 inch from the top. At the ends, space screws every 8 inches along the studs, $\frac{1}{2}$ inch from the edge.

Where an end falls at an inside corner, omit the screws, butt the next corner panel against the first, and fasten that panel to a stud. At an outside corner, lap the end of the second sheet over the first and screw the ends of both panels to the common stud.
◆ Finish the upper course of panels, then install the lower one, trimmed lengthwise to leave a $\frac{1}{2}$-inch gap at the floor. Use a foot lever to raise the panels while securing them. Stagger end joints in the courses.

Vertical wall panels.

◆ Apply adhesive to the studs to be covered by the panel *(page 83, bottom)* and lift the panel into place against the ceiling, using a pry bar on a scrap of wood as a lever.
◆ Fasten the panel to each stud with screws spaced about 2 feet apart, starting 1 inch from the top and stopping 1 inch from the bottom *(above)*.

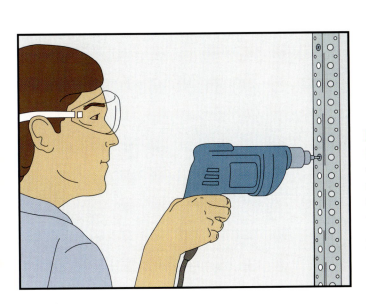

Fastening corner bead.

Protect outside corners with corner bead.
◆ Trim a strip of metal corner bead to the correct length with tin snips, cutting through one flange at a time.
◆ Position the corner bead over the wallboard joint and drive screws through its holes into the stud *(left)*.

COVERING SCREWS AND CORNER BEAD

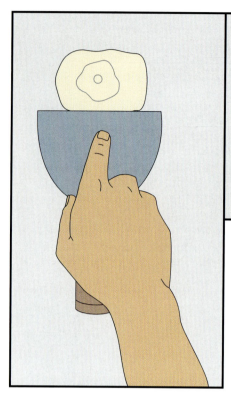

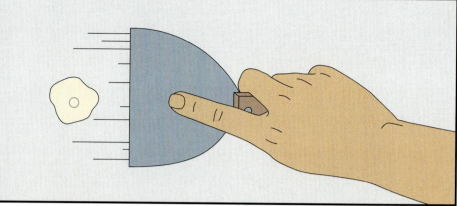

Covering fastener heads.
◆ Load half the width of a 5-inch taping knife with joint compound.
◆ Holding the blade almost parallel to the wallboard, draw the knife across the screwhead, filling the dimple completely with compound *(left)*.
◆ Raise the blade of the knife to a more upright position and scrape off excess compound with a single stroke at right angles to the first *(above)*.
◆ Apply two additional coats in the same way, letting the compound dry between applications.
◆ Once the third coat of compound dries, lightly smooth the surface with 120-grit sandpaper or a damp wallboard sponge.

Concealing corner bead.
◆ Load the left two-thirds of a 5-inch knife with joint compound.
◆ With the right 2 inches of the blade overhanging the corner, draw the knife smoothly down the left side of the corner bead *(right)*.
◆ Load the right side of the knife and run it down the right side of the bead.
◆ Scrape the knife clean, then remove excess compound and smooth the joint by drawing the blade alternately down the bead's left and right faces.
◆ Apply and smooth a second coat of compound without letting the knife overhang the corner, feathering this layer about $1\frac{1}{2}$ inches beyond the first.
◆ With an 8-inch knife, apply a third coat of compound and feather it an additional 2 inches on each side.
◆ Let the compound dry, then sand or sponge it smooth.

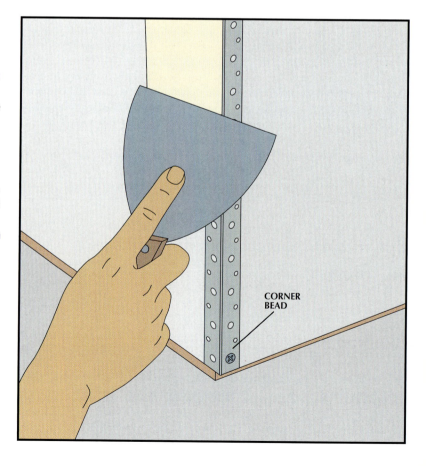

TAPING JOINTS

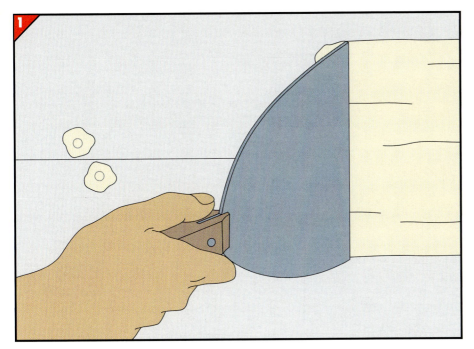

1. Applying joint compound.
◆ Load half the width of a 5-inch taping knife with joint compound.
◆ Center the blade on the joint and cock it slightly so the loaded side is the leading edge, then run the knife smoothly along the joint to fill the depression formed by the tapered edges of the panels, angling the blade gradually closer to the wallboard as you draw it along the seam *(left)*.
◆ For end-to-end joints, where the panels do not have tapered edges, apply a $\frac{1}{8}$-inch-thick layer of compound.

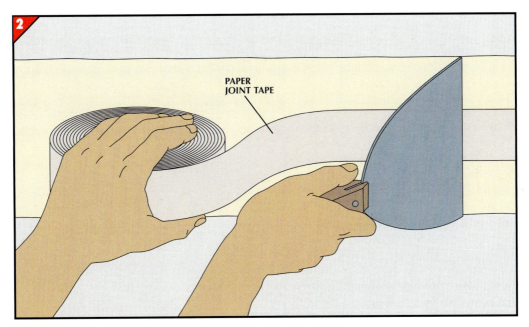

2. Embedding paper tape.
◆ Press the end of a roll of paper joint tape into the wet compound at one end of the joint.
◆ Holding the tape over the joint with one hand, run the blade of the knife along the joint to force the tape into the compound *(above)*. At the far end of the joint, tear the tape, using the knife as a straightedge.
◆ Make a second pass along the joint with the knife, pressing firmly to embed the tape in the compound and scrape off most of the excess.
◆ Make a third pass with the knife to eliminate any air bubbles.
◆ At end-to-end joints, where the tape rides on the surface, do not scrape off excess compound completely. Leave a combined tape-and-compound thickness of about $\frac{1}{8}$ inch.

DEALING WITH INSIDE CORNERS

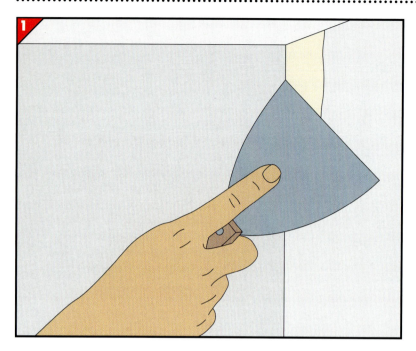

1. Putting on the compound.
◆ Load half the width of a 5-inch taping knife with joint compound.
◆ Run the knife along one side of the corner joint *(left)* and then the other, lifting the inside edge of the blade slightly to provide a thicker layer of compound at the joint. (Some of the compound may get scraped off the first side while coating the second, but this will not affect the result.)

2. Adding joint tape.
◆ Fold paper joint tape along its lengthwise crease and press it lightly into the joint compound with your fingers.
◆ Run the knife along both sides of the crease, applying just enough force for the tape to stick to the compound *(right)*.
◆ Make a second pass, pressing harder this time, to smooth the tape and squeeze out excess compound.
◆ Coat the tape lightly with some of the excess compound, then make a third pass with the knife, leaving a film of compound on the tape.

CONCEALING SEAMS

Completing flat seams.
◆ With the full width of a 10-inch knife loaded with joint compound, cover the joint tape with an even layer of the compound *(right)*.
◆ Clean the knife and draw it over the compound, holding the blade slightly off center and lifting the edge nearest the joint about $\frac{1}{8}$ inch. Make a similar pass on the other side of the joint to create a slight ridge that feathers out evenly on both sides.
◆ Let the compound dry, then lightly sand or sponge it smooth.
◆ Apply a final layer of compound with two passes of the knife: On the first pass, rest one blade edge on the center ridge and bear down on the other edge; on the second pass, repeat the procedure on the other side of the ridge.
◆ Once the compound dries, give it a final sanding or sponging.

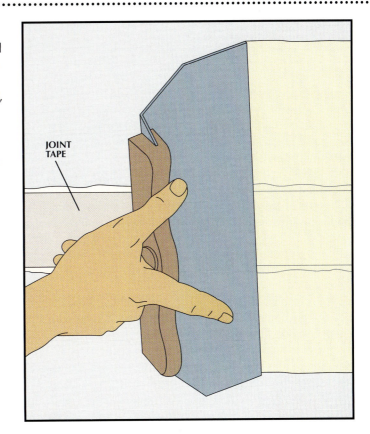

Feathering inside corners.
◆ Once both the inside-corner and wall-ceiling joints are taped, load the full width of a 5-inch taping knife and apply an even layer of compound along one side of the corner *(left)*.
◆ Scrape off any compound that laps onto the second side of the corner, then draw the knife along the first side again, bearing down on the blade's outside edge to feather the compound.
◆ Make another pass to smooth this layer, removing excess and scraping off compound left on the wall beyond the feathered edge.
◆ Let the compound dry, then feather the other side of the corner in the same way.
◆ Repeat the feathering procedure on both sides of the corner with an 8-inch knife.

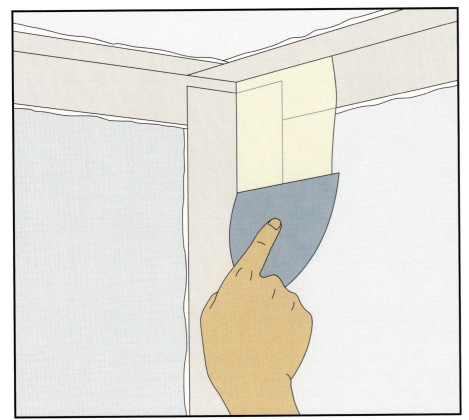

Finishing with Trim Molding

Baseboard molding covers the gap between the flooring and the wallboard and, when caulked along the floor line, also helps keep spilled liquids from infiltrating the wall or lower floors. There are two basic types from which to choose: vinyl wall base *(below)* or the more traditional wood trim *(opposite)*.

Preparing for the Job: The time to install molding is after all work on the walls and floor is finished. Smooth out irregularities at the bottom of the wall that can prevent a tight fit, such as a buildup of paint or a lump of joint compound. If you plan to paint the baseboards, you can do the walls at the same time. It is generally easier to stain baseboards after they are cut to size, but before you install them.

Vinyl wall base comes in rolls or sections, while wooden baseboards are available precut in 6- to 16-foot lengths. For a neat job, buy lengths that will minimize splices. With wood molding, add an extra couple of inches for each corner and splice, taking into account that splices must fall at studs. If you select hardwood baseboards, drill pilot holes before nailing them to prevent splitting.

Dealing with Joints: Splice two lengths of wood trim with a scarf joint *(page 92)*. Outside corners employ simple 45-degree miter cuts, but for inside corners, coped joints have the neatest appearance *(page 93)*. If one end of a piece of molding requires an angled joint, cut that end first, then square-cut the other end to fit at a corner or doorway.

TOOLS

Utility knife
Notched spreader
Heat gun
Hand roller
Electronic stud finder

C-clamps
Backsaw
Manual or power miter saw
Hammer
Nail set
Coping saw

MATERIALS

Vinyl wall base
Vinyl adhesive
Baseboard

Finishing nails (2")
Wood putty or spackling compound

SAFETY TIPS

Wear rubber gloves when applying vinyl adhesive. Protect your eyes with goggles when operating power tools or hammering.

APPLYING VINYL WALL BASE

Installing the molding.
◆ Test-fit a section of wall base along the bottom of the wall and trim it to length, if necessary, with a utility knife.
◆ With a notched spreader, coat the back of the section evenly with vinyl adhesive, applying it to within $\frac{1}{2}$ inch of the top edge *(above, left)*.

◆ Press the wall base firmly into place against the wall, ensuring that the bottom sits snugly on the flooring.
◆ To bend a section to fit around an outside or inside corner, warm it with a heat gun.
◆ Run a hand roller back and forth along the wall base to bond it to the wall *(above, right)*.

INSTALLING WOODEN BASEBOARDS

Laying out the boards.
◆ Locate the wall studs and mark their positions on the wall 6 inches or so above the flooring.
◆ Where the molding will run into door trim, butt one end into the corner and mark the board where it meets the trim *(right)*.
◆ When you must splice two pieces of baseboard for a long wall, overlap their ends at a stud and mark them for a scarf joint *(page 92, top)*.
◆ If the baseboard reaches from corner to corner, measure the wall and mark the piece to length, allowing for coped inside corner joints *(page 93)* or 45-degree miters at outside corners.

TRICKS OF THE TRADE

Fitting Baseboard to Tile Profiles

Baseboards can be fitted to the irregularities in the surface of ceramic floor tiles without painstaking scribing and cutting. By beveling the back edge of the bottom of the boards at a 45-degree angle, a thin front edge remains that, with a few taps of a hammer, conforms easily to the contours of the tiles. First run a bead of silicone caulk along the joint between the wall and floor. Position the baseboard and, protecting it with a piece of scrap wood, hit its top edge with a hammer to mold the bottom edge to the shape of the tiles, then nail it in place *(page 92, bottom)*.

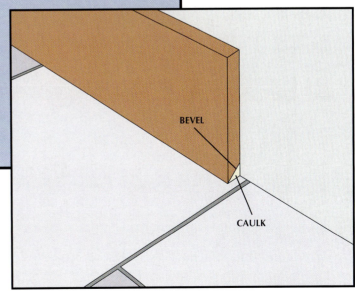

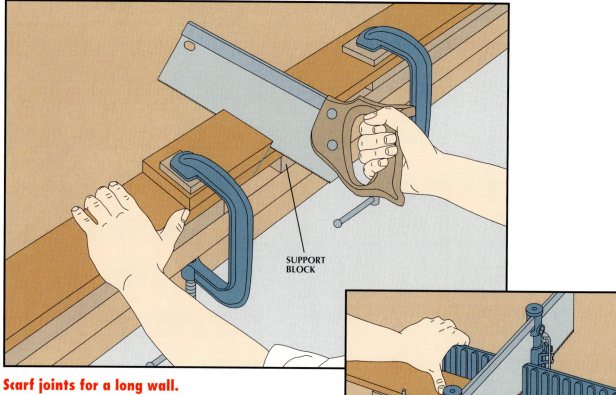

Scarf joints for a long wall.
To join two pieces of molding on a long wall, make a scarf cut for an almost invisible joint.
◆ Overlap the two adjoining pieces, set support blocks under them, and clamp the setup to a work surface.
◆ Mark a cutting line across the face of the top board and continue it at a 45-degree angle across the edges of both boards, then cut along the line with a backsaw *(above)*.
◆ With a manual or power miter saw, square-cut the ends of both pieces to fit into the corners *(inset)*.

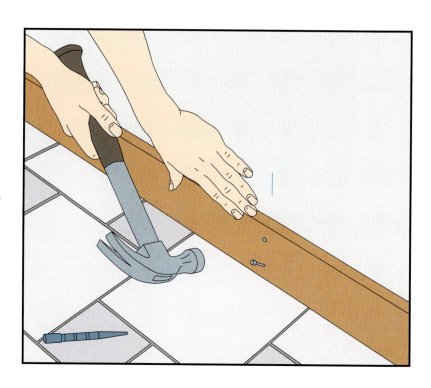

Fastening the boards.
◆ Secure baseboard to the wall by driving a pair of 2-inch finishing nails at each stud, one straight into the stud and one at an angle into the wall's soleplate *(right)*.
◆ For a scarf joint, join the ends of the pieces, centering the angled cut over the stud. On each side of the cut, drive one nail straight into the stud and another at an angle into the soleplate.
◆ Sink the nails with a nail set, then fill the holes with wood putty or, if painting the baseboards, with spackling compound.

TRICKS OF THE TRADE

Mating New Trim with Old

Whenever possible, purchase new moldings to match the existing ones in your kitchen, and join the new molding to the old with a coped joint *(below)*. In the case of an antique molding that cannot be matched, substitute a plain new molding or clear pine board cut to the same height as the old molding. Butt the end of the new molding against the inside corner, then fit the antique molding against the new molding *(right)*.

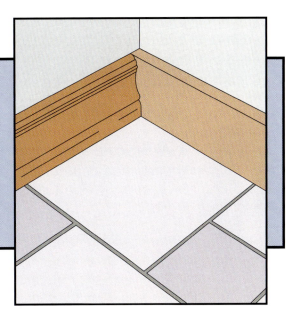

COPING CONTOURED MOLDING

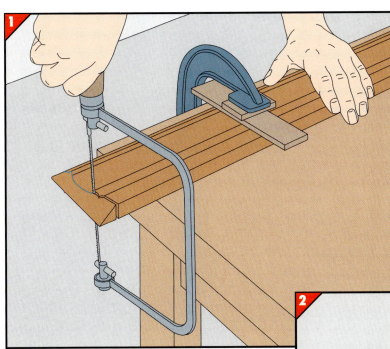

1. Cutting the molding.
◆ With a manual or power miter saw, cut the end of the molding at a 45-degree angle.
◆ Highlight the front edge of the cut with a pencil, then cut along the curve with a coping saw, angling the blade a few degrees so that the front of the molding will be a little longer than the back *(left)*.

2. Fitting the molding.
◆ Square-cut the end of the first piece of molding, butt it into the corner, and fasten it with two 2-inch finishing nails to each stud.
◆ Position the coped end of the second piece against the first *(right)*, then nail it in place.
◆ Sink the nails and fill the holes with wood putty or, if painting the baseboards, with spackling compound.

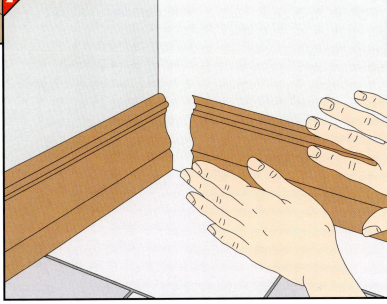

4 Cabinets and Countertops

Few upgrades can improve the appearance of a kitchen more than a new cabinet system and countertop. Whether you opt for stock or custom-made units, or plan to build European-style cabinets yourself, fitting them to the space requires precise planning and measuring. A solid-surface countertop, durable and easy to install, completes the renovation.

Installing Stock Cabinets   96

Hanging Wall Units
Fastening the Bases

A New Work Surface   103

Installing a Solid-Surface Countertop
A Tile Backsplash

Building Custom Frameless Cabinets   108

Using a Table Saw
A Circular-Saw Method
Routing Dadoes and Rabbets
Readying Cabinet Pieces

Assembling and Hanging Cabinets   116

Treating Exposed Edges
Building the Cabinets
Putting the Drawers Together
Adding Hardware
Mounting Wall Cabinets
Installing the Base Units

Leveling a base cabinet →

Installing Stock Cabinets

The most affordable kitchen cabinets are the stock units sold at home centers and lumberyards. They are available in standard dimensions, but other sizes can be specially ordered.

Choosing Cabinets: Solid wood and furniture-grade plywood generally make up the visible parts of good-quality cabinets; the bodies, shelves, and drawers are likely to be built of utilitarian plywood, hardboard, or particleboard. If the units are covered with veneer or plastic laminate, however, it may be difficult to identify the material underneath. Unless you choose unfinished units, pick cabinets that have a durable coating such as polyurethane varnish, alkyd paint, or plastic laminate. Make sure the shelves and doors are at least $\frac{3}{4}$-inch thick. The surfaces should be smooth and the edges straight; doors should hang true with snug-fitting hinges and drawers should slide smoothly in their channels.

Working Efficiently: Before installing the cabinets, remove the drawers, any adjustable shelves, and the doors—unscrewing the hinges from the frame—so they will not be in your way. Label the pieces as you remove them so they can be returned to their original locations. To install the cabinets, put in the wall units first, then the bases.

 TOOLS
Tape measure
Electronic stud finder
Carpenter's level
Stepladder
Hammer
Electric drill
C-clamps
Screwdriver
Manual or power miter saw

 MATERIALS
1 x 3s
Filler stock
Quarter-round molding
Shims
Common nails (2")
Finishing nails ($1\frac{1}{2}$")
Wood screws ($2\frac{1}{4}$", $2\frac{1}{2}$" No. 8)
Wood glue

 SAFETY TIPS
Protect your eyes with goggles when you are using power tools or hammering.

HANGING WALL UNITS

1. Marking locator lines.
◆ For a new wall, mark the studs with a tape measure *(right, top)*; for an existing wall, use the screw holes for the old cabinets, or locate the studs with a stud finder.
◆ With a carpenter's level, extend each line from the ceiling to a point that will be visible below the cabinet bottoms.
◆ Following your kitchen layout *(pages 17-18)*, draw a horizontal line with the level to mark the bottom of each cabinet *(right, bottom)*.

2. Nailing cleats.

◆ Starting at a corner or at the end of a run of cabinets, fasten a 3-foot-long 1-by-3 to the wall so its top edge aligns with the locator line *(left)*; drive a 2-inch common nail at each stud, leaving the head protruding slightly so it can be removed easily later.

◆ At a corner, nail a cleat along the locator line on the adjoining wall in the same way, butting the end of the second board against the face of the first one.

3. Positioning a corner cabinet.

◆ Working with a helper, lift the cabinet into the corner and rest it on the cleats.

◆ As the helper holds the cabinet in place, set the level against the front of the cabinet to check that the unit is vertical.

◆ Plumb the cabinet, if necessary, by tapping in shims behind it at the stud lines *(above)*.

4. Securing the cabinet.

◆ With your helper still supporting the cabinet, drill a vertical pair of countersunk holes for 2½-inch No. 8 wood screws through each of the mounting rails—the horizontal boards at the top and bottom of the cabinet back—and any shims into the studs *(right)*.
◆ Drive a screw into each hole.

5. Putting up adjacent cabinets.

◆ Remove one of the cleats that supported the corner cabinet, then fasten it to the studs *(Step 2)* for the next unit of the run.
◆ Working with your helper, lift the cabinet into position, butting its side against the corner unit *(left)*.
◆ Plumb the cabinet *(Step 3)* so its face is flush with that of the corner unit.
◆ Fasten the cabinet to the wall as you did the first unit.

6. Fastening cabinets together.

◆ Protecting the cabinets with wood pads, hold their stiles together snugly with a C-clamp or a quick-action clamp *(photograph)*, which can be installed with one hand.
◆ Drill counterbored pilot holes for 2¼-inch No. 8 wood screws through the stile of the cabinet near the top and bottom into the stile of the corner unit.
◆ Drive a screw into each hole *(right)*, then saw the shims *(page 102, Step 7)* flush with the top of the cabinets.
◆ Hang the remaining wall units in the same way as the second, adding filler strips where needed *(page 101, Step 5)*. Remove the cleats.

FASTENING THE BASES

1. Positioning the first cabinet.
◆ With a carpenter's level, extend the stud lines you marked for the wall cabinets *(page 96, Step 1)* to the floor.
◆ Position the first cabinet—in this case, a corner unit.
◆ Place the level on the front top edge of the cabinet to see whether the unit is level from side to side *(right)*. Repeat on the top edge of one of the cabinet sides to determine if it is level from front to back. If the unit is level in both directions, proceed to Step 3. Otherwise, level the cabinet *(Step 2)*.

2. Leveling the unit.
◆ With the level in position on the cabinet front, tap a shim under the base of the unit at its lowest corner, placing a wood block against the shim to help you avoid scratching the floor *(left)*.
◆ Drive in the shim until the cabinet is level.
◆ Reposition the level on the cabinet side and shim the unit if necessary.
◆ Check the cabinet for level in both directions again and adjust the shims as needed.

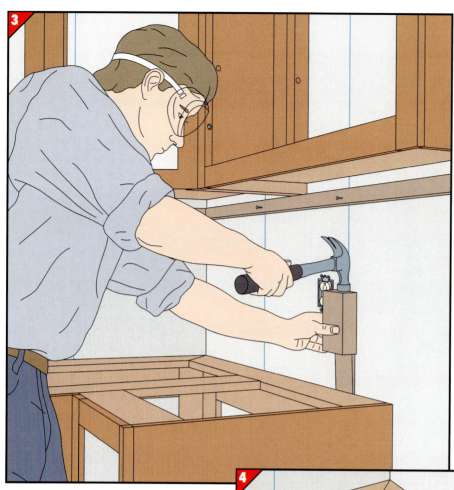

3. Shimming along the wall.
◆ If there is a gap between the back of the cabinet and the wall, slip shims into the space, centered on the studs.
◆ With a hammer and wood block, tap the shims in far enough to fit snugly without tipping the cabinet *(left)*.
◆ Check the unit for level as described in Step 2.

4. Fastening the cabinet.
◆ Drill a counterbored pilot hole for a 2½-inch No. 8 wood screw through the cabinet's mounting rail into each stud; if there are shims between the unit and the wall, drill through them.
◆ Drive a screw into each hole *(right)*.
◆ Check the cabinet for level *(page 99, Step 1)*, then loosen the screws and adjust shims as necessary to level the unit.

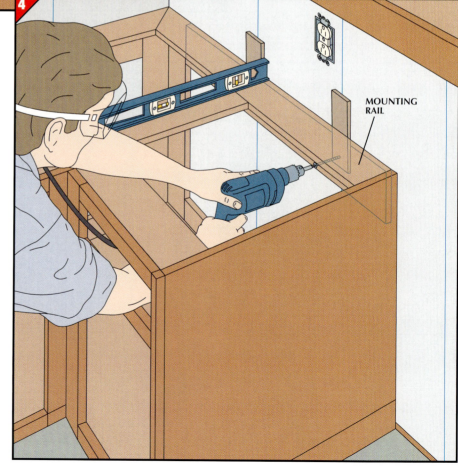

MOUNTING RAIL

5. Attaching a filler strip.

◆ Where your kitchen layout *(pages 17-18)* calls for a filler strip, glue and clamp the strip to the stile of the next cabinet to be installed, so the faces of the stile and filler strip are flush; protect the unit and strip with wood pads.
◆ Drill counterbored pilot holes for $2\frac{1}{2}$-inch No. 8 wood screws through the stile near the top and bottom into the filler strip.
◆ Drive a screw into each hole *(right)*.

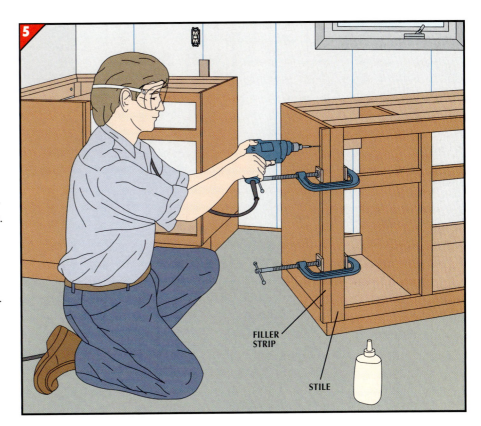

6. Installing the second cabinet.

◆ Remove the clamps from the unit with the filler strip and slide it into position, butting the edge of the strip against the corner cabinet.
◆ Level the unit and fasten it to the wall as you did the first one *(Steps 2-4)*.
◆ Clamp the stiles of the cabinets together snugly and drill two counterbored pilot holes through the stile of the corner unit into the filler strip, keeping the holes away from the screws holding the strip to the adjoining cabinet.
◆ Drive the screws *(above)*.
◆ Install the remaining base cabinets.

101

7. Trimming the shims.
◆ Holding a backsaw at an angle and taking care not to mar the cabinet, cut almost all the way through the shims at the bottom of the cabinet *(right)*. Stop short of the floor to avoid damaging its surface.
◆ Snap off the excess pieces of shim.
◆ Follow the same procedure to trim the wall shims at the tops of the cabinets.

8. Adding molding.
◆ Cut a strip of quarter-round molding to run along the kick plate of each run of base cabinets. Miter ends that meet at corners at 45 degrees, using a manual or power miter saw; at a wall or appliance, cut the molding square, in line with the end of the cabinet.
◆ Holding the strip flush against the kick plate, fasten it to the floor with $1\frac{1}{2}$-inch finishing nails driven at 16-inch intervals *(left)*.
◆ Install the countertop for the base cabinets *(pages 103-107)*.

A New Work Surface

The ideal countertop is easy to install and tough enough to withstand an endless succession of assaults by liquids, knife cuts, dropped pots, and hot cookware. The solid-surface variety is a good choice, being more durable than plastic laminate, less expensive than granite, and easier to install than tile.

Ordering: A solid-surface countertop can be custom-made to fit your cabinets, and comes with or without a backsplash and curved front edge. Order it to overhang the front and sides of the base cabinets by about $1\frac{1}{2}$ inches. Provide the dealer with a template of the sink so the hole can be precut. Turn the sink upside down on a piece of cardboard, trace its contour, then cut out the template.

Installation: First, furring strips are screwed to the base cabinets to support the counter *(below)*. The top is held down with silicone caulk rather than screws, and a slight gap is left where it meets an end wall.

Once the counter is in place, install the sink: Apply plumber's putty or the sealant provided by the sink manufacturer around the opening for the sink, set the basin into position, and fasten it to the countertop from below with the lug bolts or clamps provided. Reconnect the plumbing *(page 24)*.

If the countertop has no curved front edge, nail molding across the ends of the furring strips to conceal them. For a top without a backsplash, you can fashion one of ceramic tile to add a decorative accent *(page 107)*.

 TOOLS

Electric drill
Compass
Belt sander
Caulking gun
C-clamps
Glue gun
Handscrew
   clamps
Block plane
Random-orbit
   sander
Electronic stud
   finder
Tile cutter
Notched spreader
Grout float
Manual or power
   miter saw

 MATERIALS

1 x 1s, 1 x 4s
Plywood ($\frac{1}{8}$", $\frac{1}{2}$")
Wood screws ($1\frac{1}{4}$", $1\frac{1}{2}$"
   No. 8)
Finishing nails ($1\frac{1}{2}$")
Silicone caulk
Aluminum
   conductive tape
Solid-surface joint
   adhesive
Polishing pad
Hot-melt glue
Ceramic tiles
Masking tape
Thin-set mortar
Epoxy grout
Quarter-round molding
Wood glue

 SAFETY TIPS

Wear goggles when sawing, sanding, or hammering.

INSTALLING A SOLID-SURFACE COUNTERTOP

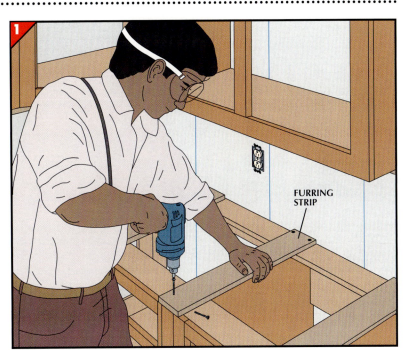

1. Installing furring strips.
◆ Cut a piece of 1-by-4 to the depth of the cabinets.
◆ Set the strip across the first cabinet at one end of the run and fasten it in place with four $1\frac{1}{4}$-inch No. 8 wood screws.
◆ Cut and install a furring strip every 18 inches along the cabinet run *(right)*. Center an additional strip where two sections of countertop will be joined *(page 105, Step 5)* and add strips 3 inches to each side of an opening for a sink or built-in cooktop.

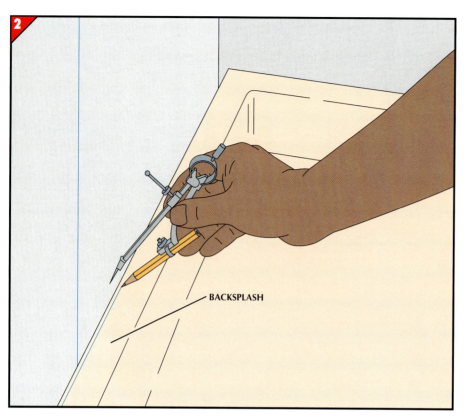

2. Test-fitting the countertop.
◆ With a helper, position the countertop on the cabinets, butting it against the back wall. If there is more than one countertop section, make sure all their front edges are flush.
◆ If an uneven wall surface causes gaps wider than $\frac{1}{16}$ inch between the counter and the wall, set a compass to a distance slightly wider than the largest gap, and holding the compass almost horizontal and running the point along the wall, scribe a line along the counter *(left)*.

3. Sanding the backsplash.
◆ Clamp the countertop to a work bench, protecting the surface with wood pads.
◆ Run a belt sander fitted with a coarse belt along the back of the counter, angling the tool to remove slightly more material from the bottom edge than the top *(right)*. Sand the surface down to the line.

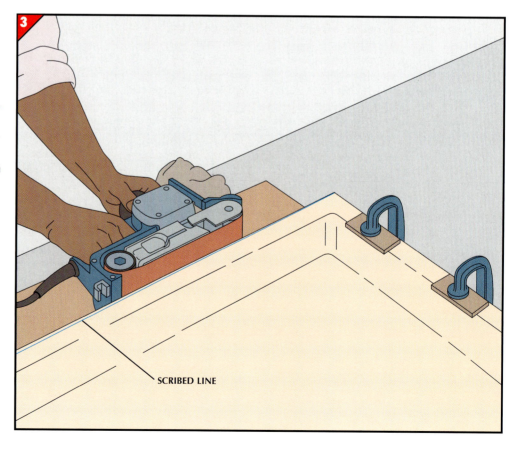

4. Applying caulk.

◆ Where two countertop sections will be joined, apply aluminum conductive tape along the length of the furring strip located directly below the seam.
◆ With a caulking gun, apply a dab of silicone caulk every 8 inches along each furring or tape strip *(right)*.

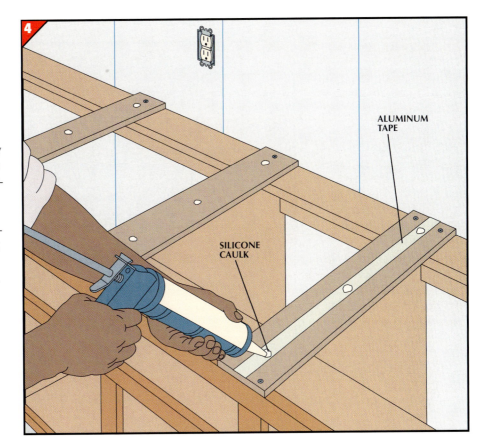

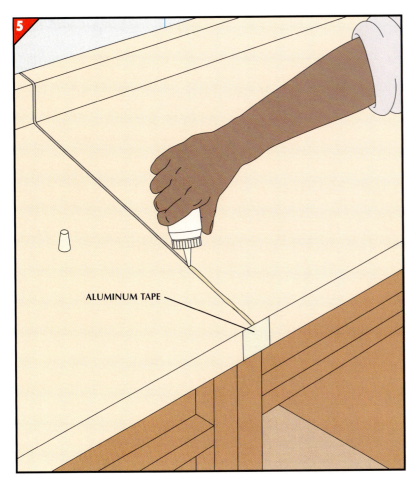

5. Preparing countertop seams.

◆ With a helper, reposition a section of countertop on the cabinets. Anchor the section to the furring strips with C-clamps.
◆ Set the adjoining section on the cabinets so there is an even gap of $\frac{1}{16}$ inch between the two sections and their front edges are flush.
◆ Cover the gap along the front edge and under the overhang with aluminum tape.
◆ Starting at the front of the seam, run a tube of solid-surface joint adhesive in a matching color along the joint, filling the gap half full *(left)*.
◆ Push the second section against the first until a bead of adhesive squeezes out of the seam along its length. Pop any air bubbles with a toothpick and add adhesive to areas where it is below the surface of the countertop.

6. Clamping the seam.
◆ With a glue gun, run beads of hot-melt glue 1½ inches on each side of the seam and attach a 1-by-1 wood cleat 1 inch to each side of the joint.
◆ Let the glue set for a few minutes, then tighten two handscrew clamps on the cleats to pull the two sections snugly together *(right)*.
◆ Allow the joint adhesive to cure for about an hour, then remove the clamps and knock off the cleats with a hammer.
◆ Remove any residual glue using a putty knife with rounded edges.

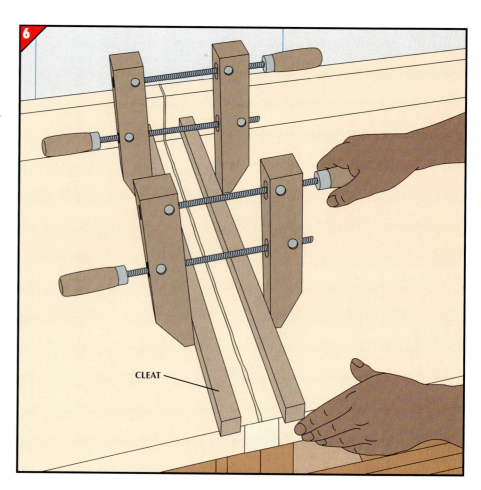

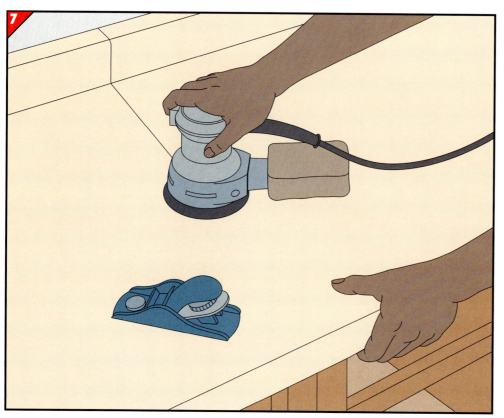

7. Smoothing the seam.
◆ Shave off excess joint adhesive with a block plane, taking care not to gouge the surface.
◆ Smooth the joint using a random-orbit sander fitted with a medium sanding pad *(left)*.
◆ Fit the sander with a synthetic polishing pad and buff the entire countertop surface.

A TILE BACKSPLASH

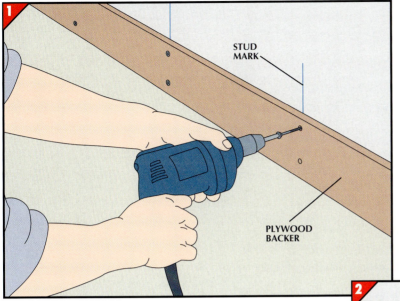

1. Attaching a plywood backer.
◆ Cut $\frac{1}{2}$-inch plywood $\frac{1}{4}$ inch wider than the height of the backsplash tiles to the length of the countertop; subtract $\frac{1}{4}$ inch from this distance for each end of the backsplash that does not meet a wall and will be trimmed with molding *(Step 3)*.
◆ Locate wall studs along the countertop with an electronic stud finder and mark them.
◆ Set the plywood against the wall as a backer for the tiles and fasten it to the wall *(left)*, driving two $1\frac{1}{2}$-inch No. 8 wood screws at each stud.

2. Laying the tiles.
◆ Lay out a dry run of tiles along the length of the backer, separating them with $\frac{1}{8}$-inch plywood spacers. If tiles need to be cut to fit exactly, use a tile cutter *(page 81, Step 6)* to trim the same amount from the two tiles at the ends of the run. If the backsplash meets an adjacent wall, leave space for a joint at the wall.
◆ Wipe the backer with a damp cloth and apply masking tape along the back edge of the countertop.
◆ With a notched spreader, apply a ridged bed of thin-set mortar to the first 2 feet of the backer.
◆ Place two spacers on the masking-tape strip at the first tile location, set the tile on the spacers, and press it into the adhesive, twisting it back and forth to ensure a proper bond.
◆ Lay the remaining tiles in the same way, separating them with two spacers *(right)*.

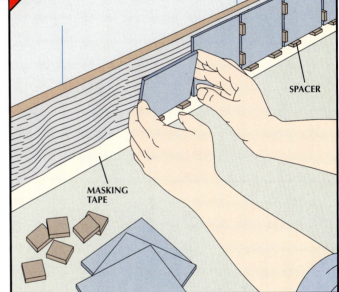

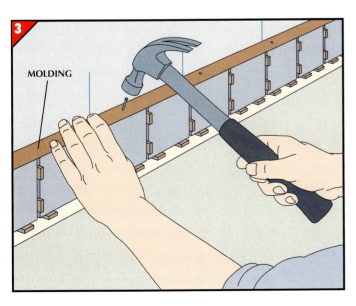

3. Attaching molding.
◆ Buy quarter-round molding with a radius equal to the combined thickness of the backer and the tile. Cut the molding to fit along the exposed edges of the backer, mitering ends at 45 degrees for joints at inside corners or on vertical pieces.
◆ Spread wood glue on the back of the molding, position it along the top edge of the backer, and fasten it to the wall with $1\frac{1}{2}$-inch finishing nails spaced 6 inches apart *(left)*.
◆ Cut and fasten vertical strips of molding along any open ends of the backsplash in the same way.
◆ Remove the tile spacers and fill the joints with epoxy grout *(page 81, Step 7)*. Apply a sealer to unglazed tiles.

Building Custom Frameless Cabinets

Building your own kitchen cabinets can be much less expensive than ordering custom-made units. Frameless, or European-style, cabinets *(page 17 and opposite)* are one of the most practical types—not only are they easy to construct and install, but you can adapt them to different uses by arranging the shelves and drawers as you please.

Materials: If you plan to stain the cabinets, build the units of cabinet-grade plywood or veneer-laminated particleboard. For added elegance—and at greater cost—you can make the visible parts from solid wood such as cherry or maple. When cabinets will be painted, medium-density fiberboard (MDF) is a less expensive option. You can also use plastic laminates, which come in a variety of colors. Make the inside parts of the drawers from a less costly material such as common plywood and the bottoms from $\frac{1}{4}$-inch hardboard. For all other materials, choose $\frac{3}{4}$-inch-thick stock.

Planning the Job: First, sketch the layout to plan the positions and types of cabinets you want *(pages 17-18)*. To economize on materials, draw a cutting diagram before you begin *(page 110)*.

TOOLS

Table saw
Roller stand
C-clamps
Electric drill
Countersink bit
Screwdriver bit
Circular saw
Plunge router
Straight bit ($\frac{3}{4}$")
Hole-drilling jig, guide, and 5-mm brad-point bit
Dowel centers
Rubber mallet
Self-centering dowel jig
Spade bit (1")
Brad-point bit ($\frac{5}{16}$")
Hinge-drilling jig and 35-mm Forstner bit

MATERIALS

Graph paper
1 x 3
Cabinet stock
Wood screws ($1\frac{1}{4}$" No. 8)

 SAFETY TIPS

When working with a power tool, wear goggles to protect your eyes.

JIGS FOR EUROCABINET CONSTRUCTION

Specialized jigs, guides, and bits make it easy to position and drill the holes required for Eurocabinet construction. The tools are sized in millimeters (mm) rather than inches, and are readily available from a woodworking specialty shop or catalog, as are the 5-mm dowels and shelf pins that fit the holes.

The hole-drilling jig has two functions. One side is used to position holes at the correct intervals for the screws and dowels that fasten the cabinet parts together. The opposite side spaces holes for the pins that support the adjustable shelves. The 5-mm carbide-tipped brad-point bit used to drill the holes is fitted into a self-centering drill guide to ensure that the holes are straight, centered within the jig's holes, and bored to the correct depth.

For situating holes for Eurohinges, the hinge-drilling jig has a guide fence and a swivel stop that butt up against the edges of the panels. A 35-mm Forstner bit fits into the shaft assembly in the center of the jig.

The self-centering dowel jig is employed to position holes for dowels in the edges of panels. It is clamped over an edge and aligned over the hole location. A 5-mm brad-point bit fitted with a stop collar is inserted into the jig to bore the holes to a precise depth.

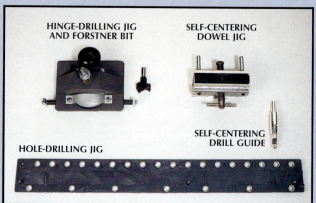

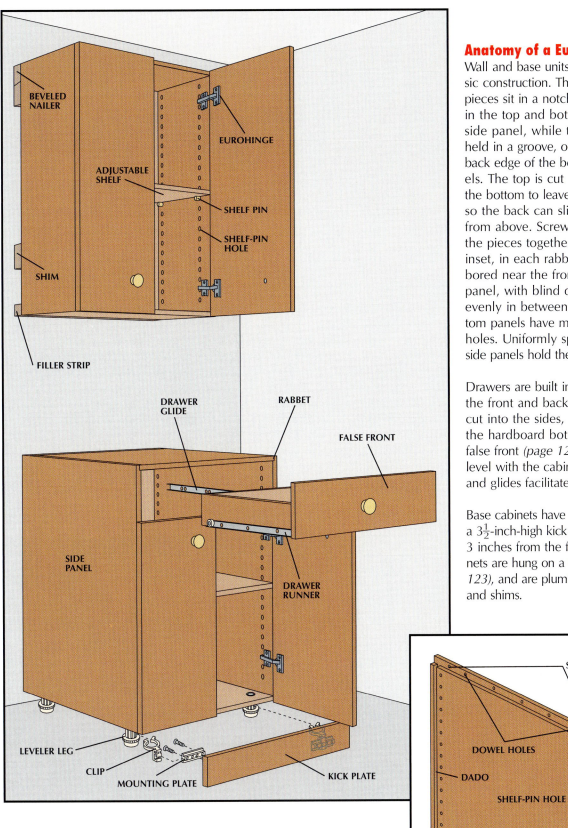

Anatomy of a Eurocabinet.

Wall and base units have the same basic construction. The top and bottom pieces sit in a notch, or rabbet, routed in the top and bottom edges of each side panel, while the back piece is held in a groove, or dado, cut near the back edge of the bottom and side panels. The top is cut 1 inch shorter than the bottom to leave a space at the rear so the back can slide into the dadoes from above. Screws and dowels hold the pieces together. As shown in the inset, in each rabbet, screw holes are bored near the front and back of the panel, with blind dowel holes spaced evenly in between; the top and bottom panels have matching blind dowel holes. Uniformly spaced holes in the side panels hold the shelf pins.

Drawers are built in a similar way, with the front and back fitting into rabbets cut into the sides, and a dado holding the hardboard bottom *(page 119)*. A false front *(page 122)* brings the drawer level with the cabinet top, and runners and glides facilitate its movements.

Base cabinets have adjustable legs and a $3\frac{1}{2}$-inch-high kick plate that is recessed 3 inches from the front. The wall cabinets are hung on a beveled nailer *(page 123)*, and are plumbed using filler strips and shims.

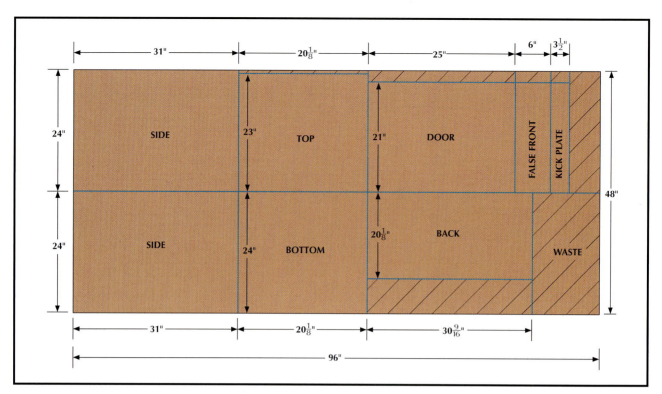

Cutting the pieces.

To economize on wood, make a diagram to lay out the sides, back, top and bottom, doors, false drawer fronts, and kick plates for each cabinet. For the drawer, make the sides, back, and front from a less expensive material, and the bottom from $\frac{1}{4}$-inch hardboard. The example above is for a base unit measuring $34\frac{1}{2}$ inches high, 24 inches deep, and 21 inches wide, made of $\frac{3}{4}$-inch stock.

◆ Trim a piece of graph paper to the scale of the cabinet stock, with each grid square representing a specific number of inches. Using the same scale, cut pieces from another sheet of graph paper to represent each part of the cabinet.

◆ Arrange the pieces on the first graph so they produce the least possible waste, placing them so that the first cuts on the saw are straight lines along the length of the sheet. Add an extra $\frac{1}{8}$ inch or so to allow for the saw kerf.

◆ Trace the shapes onto the first sheet of paper, then transfer them to the wood *(above)*. As you cut each piece, remeasure before cutting the next.

USING A TABLE SAW

1. Ripping a panel.

◆ Adjust the rip fence so the distance between it and the blade equals the width of the cut along the length of the panel.
◆ Position a roller stand beside the saw table to help support the panel.
◆ Working with a helper, set the leading end of the panel on the table a few inches from the blade, pressing the edge against the fence *(right)*.
◆ Slowly feed the panel into the blade, raising the trailing end slightly to keep the front end level.
◆ Keeping your hands on each side of the blade and well clear of it, continue feeding the panel into the blade until the cut is completed.

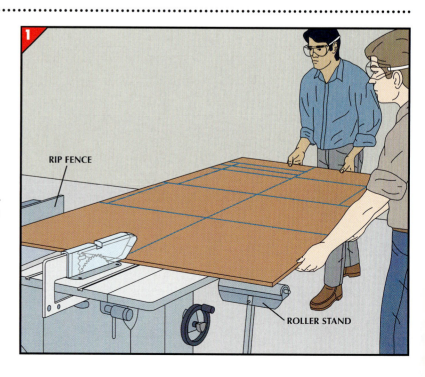

A Shop-Built Roller Stand

Combined with two C-clamps, some wood, and a commercial roller, a wooden sawhorse can serve as an effective roller stand that is cheaper than a store-bought model. Make a T-shaped mast for the roller from two pieces of 2-by-4 stock, ensuring it is tall enough to hold the roller slightly below the level of the saw table. Screw the roller to the mast and clamp the mast to the sawhorse braces so the roller is horizontal.

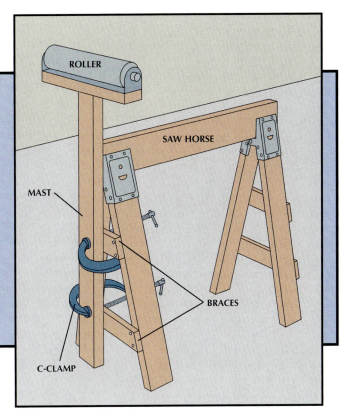

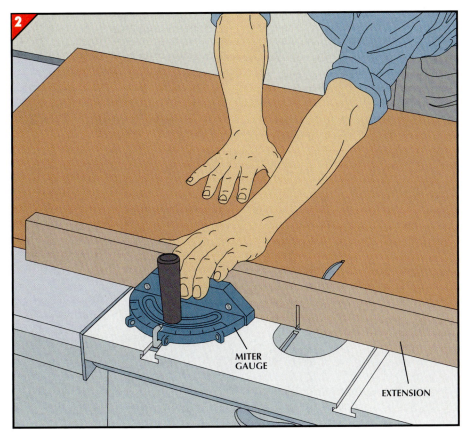

2. Crosscutting.

◆ For a panel that is wider than the distance between the front edge of the table and the saw blade, the miter gauge cannot be used in its usual position—in front of the blade—to begin the cut. Instead, insert the gauge in its slot from the back of the table. For extra stability, screw a 4-foot-long 1-by-3 as an extension to the gauge.

◆ Hold the extension with one hand while pressing the workpiece against it with the other. Feed the piece into the blade *(left)* until the trailing end of the panel reaches the front of the table. *(In the illustration, the blade guard has been removed for clarity.)*

◆ Turn off the saw, slide the miter gauge out of its slot, reinsert it from the front of the table, and complete the cut.

A CIRCULAR-SAW METHOD

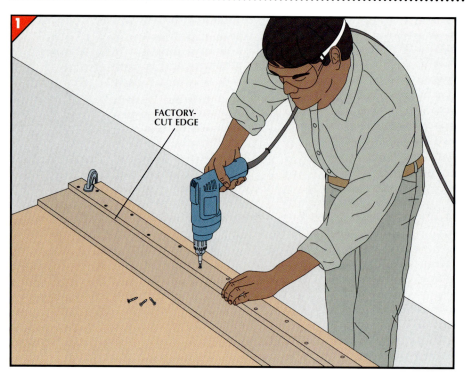

1. Making an edge guide.
◆ Cut a $2\frac{1}{4}$-inch-wide strip from the factory-cut edge of a $\frac{3}{4}$-inch plywood panel. Cut a second length, this one wider than the first by an amount equal to the distance between the blade of the circular saw and the outside of the saw's base plate—typically, 5 inches.
◆ Align the two strips so the factory-cut edge of the narrow piece divides the width of the wider one. Clamp the strips to a work surface.
◆ Countersink pilot holes for $1\frac{1}{4}$-inch No. 8 wood screws in a W pattern along the edges of the narrow strip, then fasten the pieces together *(left)*.

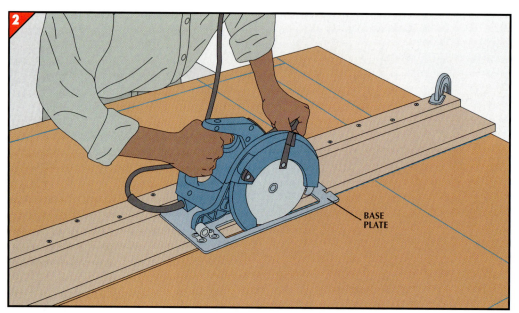

2. Ripping a panel.
◆ Transfer the cutting lines for the cabinet pieces to the back of the panel, then clamp the panel good-face down to a work surface so the first cutting line overhangs the table.
◆ Clamp the edge guide to the panel so the edge of the wider strip aligns with the cutting line.
◆ Adjust the blade depth to the combined thickness of the guide and the panel.
◆ Riding the saw's base plate along the factory-cut edge of the narrow strip, cut the panel *(above)*. When the saw is about 12 inches from the end of the cut, have a helper support the waste piece to keep it from breaking off before the cut is completed.

ROUTING DADOES AND RABBETS

Preparing the panels.
◆ To outline the rabbets at the top and bottom of each side panel, draw a line $\frac{3}{4}$ inch from the edge on the inner surface of the wood.
◆ For the dadoes that hold the back panel in place, outline a $\frac{3}{4}$-inch groove $\frac{1}{4}$ inch from the back edges of the side panels. Mark an identical groove $\frac{1}{4}$ inch from the back edge of the bottom panel.
◆ Equip a plunge router with a $\frac{3}{4}$-inch-wide straight bit, center the bit over one of the outlines near one end of the panel, and mark the edge of the router's base plate on the panel *(right)*. Repeat the process near the opposite end of the panel and join the marks to provide a reference line for an edge guide.
◆ Draw a similar reference line for the other dadoes and rabbets.

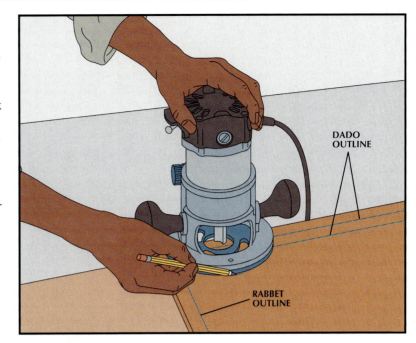

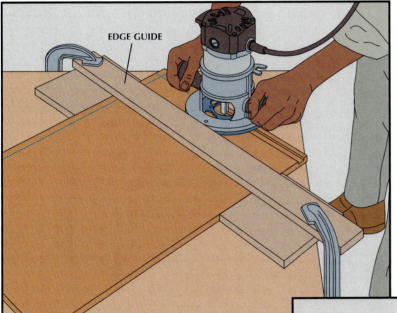

Cutting a dado.
◆ Set a side panel on a work surface and lay a straight board as an edge guide along one of the lines you marked above. Support the guide on wood blocks to keep it from tipping and clamp it securely.
◆ Adjust the bit depth to $\frac{5}{16}$ inch and hold the router above the wood at one end of the dado outline, resting the base plate against the edge guide.
◆ Turn the router on, press down on the handles to plunge the bit into the wood, and ease the tool along the guide *(left)* until the cut is finished.

Routing a rabbet.
◆ Reposition the panel and the edge guide to align the router bit with the rabbet outline.
◆ Cut the rabbet as you would a dado *(right)*.

113

READYING CABINET PIECES

1. Drilling the first holes.
◆ Lay a side panel inside face up on a work surface, aligning the top with the edge of the table.
◆ Place a hole-drilling jig *(page 108)* flush with the top and front of the panel, then clamp it down, protecting it with wood pads.
◆ Fit a 5-mm carbide-tipped brad-point bit in a self-centering drill guide *(page 108)* and attach it to an electric drill. Starting at the front of the panel, push the guide into each of the holes along the outer edge of the jig to drill the screw and dowel holes *(right)*. If the screw hole at the back of the panel will interfere with the dado, do not drill it. Remove the jig, measure in $\frac{1}{2}$ inch from the dado, and drill a screw hole there.
◆ Turn the panel over, realign the jig, and finish drilling the two screw holes all the way through the panel, measuring to find the position of the hole near the dado if necessary.
◆ Repeat the process to drill the holes along the bottom rabbet, then follow the same procedure with the jig aligned along the sides of the panel to drill the shelf-pin holes.

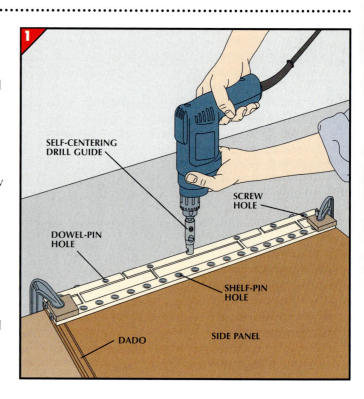

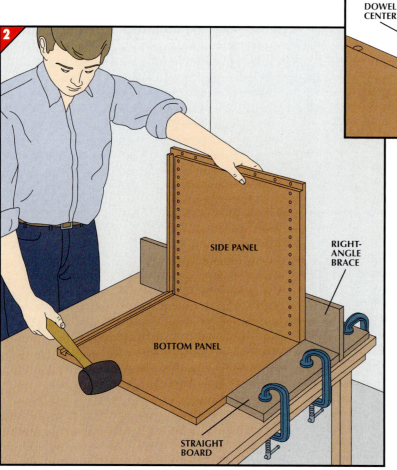

2. Drilling matching dowel holes.
◆ Make a right-angle brace by fastening two boards together at a 90-degree angle. Clamp the brace to a work surface; then clamp a straight board to the work table perpendicular to the brace.
◆ Insert a dowel center into each of the holes drilled in one of the side panels *(inset)*.
◆ Hold the side panel upright against the brace with the dowel centers at the bottom, then set the bottom panel flat on the table.
◆ Tap the bottom panel with a rubber mallet, driving the dowel-center points into the bottom panel *(left)*.
◆ Place a self-centering dowel jig *(page 108)* over each dowel-center mark in the bottom panel and bore the holes with a 5-mm bit.
◆ Repeat the process to make matching dowel holes in the other edges of the bottom panel, as well as in both edges of the top panel.

3. Preparing bottom panels for base levelers.

◆ Place the bottom panel face up on a work surface and mark a line across it 3 inches from the front edge to represent the kick plate.
◆ At each corner of the panel, measure in $2\frac{3}{4}$ inches from the side and from the back edge or kick-plate line, marking points for the bolts that secure the levelers to the panel *(right)*.
◆ Place a scrap panel under the workpiece and drill the holes for the bolts in three stages: Start with a $\frac{1}{8}$-inch pilot hole right through the panel, then, with a 1-inch spade bit, drill a hole $\frac{1}{4}$ inch deep, using the pilot hole to center the bit. Switch to a $\frac{5}{16}$-inch brad-point bit and drill completely through the panel.

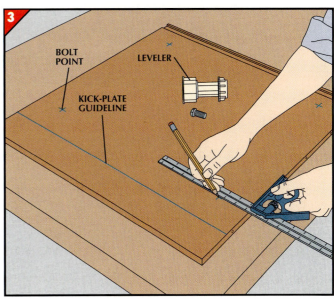

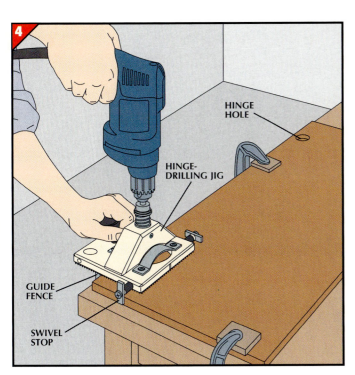

4. Drilling holes for European hinges.

◆ Clamp the door face up to the work surface and insert a 35-mm Forstner bit in the guide shaft of a hinge-drilling jig *(page 108)*.
◆ Place the jig on the door so its guide fence is flush against the door's hinge edge and the swivel stop rests on the top end of the door. Attach an electric drill to the jig and press down to bore the hinge hole—the jig ensures that the hole will be the correct depth.
◆ Reposition the jig and drill at the bottom of the door and bore the second hole *(left)*.

TRICKS OF THE TRADE

A Shelf-Pin-Hole Jig

In lieu of a commercial jig *(opposite, Step 1)*, you can drill a row of evenly spaced shelf-pin holes with a jig made from two pieces of wood. Fasten 8- and 24-inch lengths of 1-by-3 stock together into a T shape so they form a 90-degree angle. Mark a line down the middle of the longer piece, then drill holes through it at 32-mm intervals. Clamp the jig to a cabinet panel so the T is flush against the top or bottom and the centerline on the long piece is 2 inches from the edge. Fit the bit with a stop collar set to include the hole depth and the thickness of the jig, and drill the holes *(right)*.

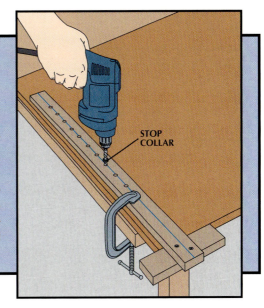

Assembling and Hanging Cabinets

Cabinets and drawers are all assembled with screws and dowels in a uniform size: $1\frac{1}{4}$-inch No. 8 wood screws and 5-mm dowels *(below)*. The uniformity of the system also makes the installation of drawer glides and doors *(pages 119-122)* straightforward. Before putting the units together, cover exposed plywood edges with edge banding *(below)*.

An Alternate Assembly: You can install the fasteners to facilitate disassembly of the cabinets, if desired: When inserting the dowels into the panels, spread glue on only one end; in doing so, the mating panel will not bond to the dowel when the panels are fitted together.

Finishing the Cabinets: The simplest way to conceal screwheads after the cabinets are assembled is by filling the recesses: Use spackling compound if you will be painting the units, or wood putty where you plan to apply a clear finish.

Hanging the Units: European-style cabinets are installed securely, but can be unmounted easily. Base cabinets sit on levelers that both support the units and keep them level *(page 125)*, and in the installation method shown on these pages, wall units are hung with matching nailer boards that are fastened to the wall and cabinets, but not to each other *(pages 123-124)*.

**TOOLS**

Household iron
Hand roller
File
Wood chisel
C-clamps
Bar clamp
Handscrew clamps
Electric drill
Carpenter's square
Angle clamp
Plunge router
Straight bit ($\frac{3}{4}$")
Combination square
Chalk line
Table saw
Socket wrench
Carpenter's level

MATERIALS

Edge banding
Wood strips ($\frac{1}{2}$" x 1")
1 x 1s, 1 x 3s, 1 x 6s
Plywood ($\frac{1}{4}$")
Finishing nails (1")
Fluted dowels (5 mm)
Wood glue

Wood screws ($1\frac{1}{4}$", $1\frac{1}{2}$", $1\frac{3}{4}$", 3" No. 8)
Bolts (5 mm), washers, nuts
Drawer runners and glides
Eurohinges
Door and drawer handles
Base levelers
Kick-plate mounting plate

SAFETY TIPS

Protect your eyes with goggles when you are using a power tool.

TREATING EXPOSED EDGES

1. Applying edge banding.
◆ Support the panel vertically with clamps, and set a household iron to HIGH (without steam).
◆ Cut a strip of commercial edge banding slightly longer than the edge to be covered and place the strip on the edge with the adhesive side down.
◆ Run the hot iron slowly along the edge, pressing the banding flat; to prevent scorching the material, avoid holding the iron in one spot for more than a few seconds.
◆ Applying even pressure, run a hand roller back and forth over the edge *(right)*.

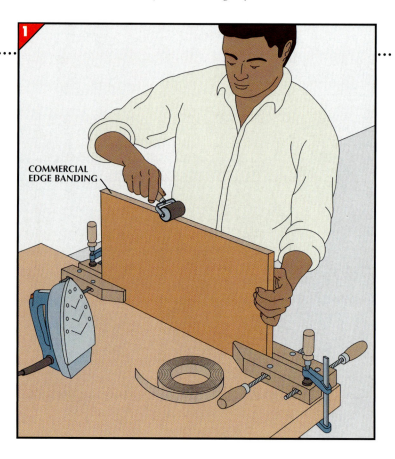

2. Trimming the banding.

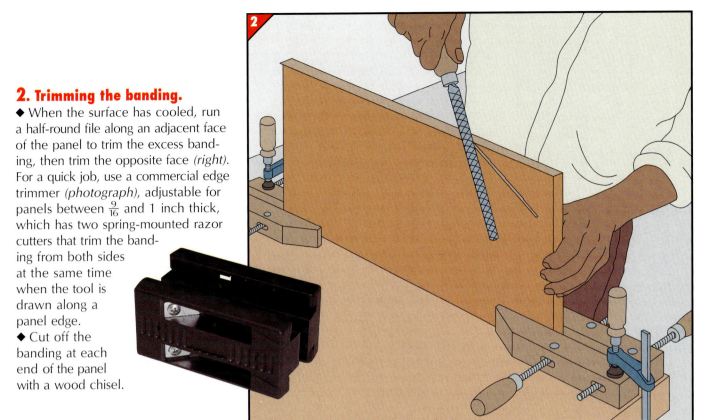

◆ When the surface has cooled, run a half-round file along an adjacent face of the panel to trim the excess banding, then trim the opposite face *(right)*. For a quick job, use a commercial edge trimmer *(photograph)*, adjustable for panels between $\frac{9}{16}$ and 1 inch thick, which has two spring-mounted razor cutters that trim the banding from both sides at the same time when the tool is drawn along a panel edge.
◆ Cut off the banding at each end of the panel with a wood chisel.

BUILDING THE CABINETS

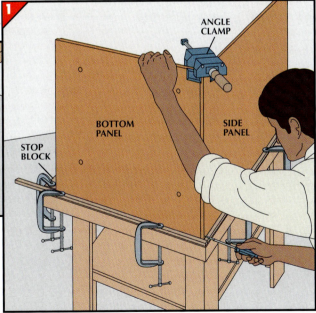

1. Fastening the top and bottom to the sides.
◆ Make a simple jig to help you fasten cabinet panels at a 90-degree angle to each other: Clamp two $\frac{1}{2}$-inch-high, 1-inch-wide wood strips along adjoining edges of your workbench, using a carpenter's square to make sure the strips form a right angle where the end of one meets the edge of the other *(inset)*.
◆ For each dowel hole along one edge of a side panel, spread wood glue on one end of a 5-mm fluted dowel and insert the dowel into the hole.
◆ Stand the panel on the bench flush against one of the jig strips so the dowels are at the corner, and position the bottom panel against the adjoining strip, fitting the projecting dowels into its holes.
◆ Install an angle clamp at the top of the joint to keep the panels at right angles to each other. Use the carpenter's square to maintain the angle at the bottom.
◆ Clamp a stop block to the bench to keep the bottom panel from moving, then drill pilot holes for $1\frac{1}{2}$-inch No. 8 wood screws into the bottom panel through the holes that were already drilled in the side panel.
◆ Drive a screw into each hole *(above)*.
◆ Fasten the top and remaining side panel together in the same way.

2. Putting the two sides together.
◆ Place the two assemblies on the bench so one of the corners to be fastened is seated in the jig. Secure the opposite corner with the angle clamp.
◆ Screw the assemblies together *(right)*, as described in Step 1.

3. Adding the back panel.
◆ Place the cabinet right-side up on the floor and slide the back panel into its dadoes in the side and bottom panels *(left)*.
◆ Drill pilot holes at the top and bottom of the side panels, centering them over the edge of the back panel, then screw the back to the side panels through the holes.

PUTTING THE DRAWERS TOGETHER

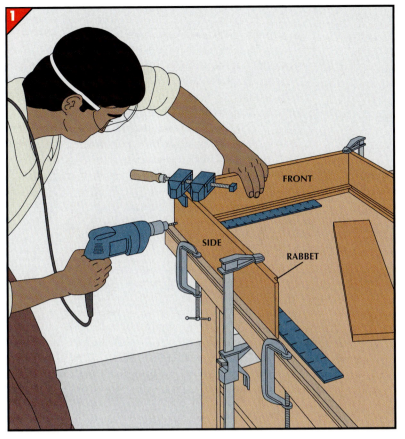

1. Assembling the drawers.
◆ Cut the drawer parts to fit the cabinets, taking into account the hardware that connects the drawers to the cabinet sides. Make the back of the drawers $\frac{1}{2}$ inch shorter in height than the sides and front.
◆ Rout the drawers as you did the cabinets *(page 113)*, cutting rabbets in the side pieces and dadoes in the sides and front to accommodate the bottom, but make the dadoes $\frac{1}{4}$ inch wide to accommodate the $\frac{1}{4}$-inch hardboard bottom.
◆ Fasten the front to one side and then the other *(left)*. Since the drawer sides are shorter than the cabinet sides, you can secure them upright to your bench with bar clamps rather than use a stop block.
◆ Rotate the assembly 180 degrees on the bench, then add the back, fitting it into its rabbets in the sides.
◆ Fit the hardboard bottom in the dadoes *(opposite, Step 3)* and fasten it to the bottom edge of the back with three 1-inch finishing nails.

2. Fastening drawer runners.
◆ Place the drawer upside down on the work surface and position a drawer runner on the side so its front end is flush with the drawer front.
◆ Mark each screw hole, remove the runner, and drill pilot holes for the screws supplied at the marks.
◆ Fasten the runner to the drawer.
◆ Attach a runner to the opposite side in the same manner *(right)*.

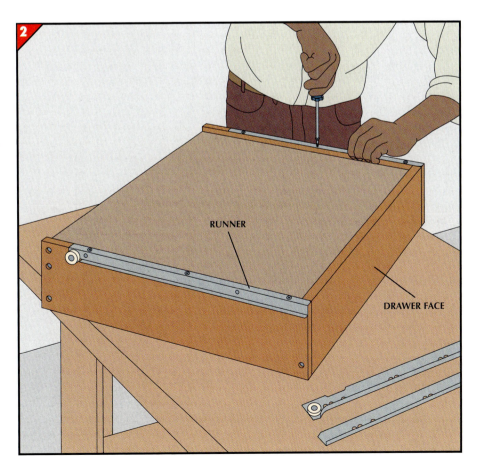

ADDING HARDWARE

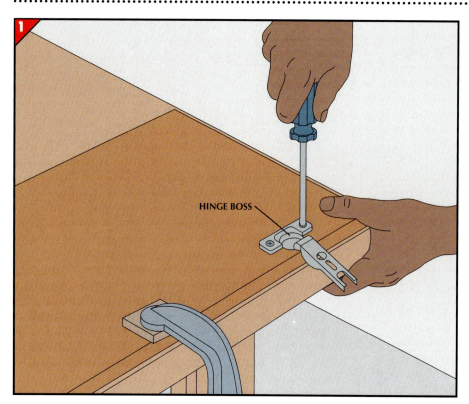

1. Attaching hinges to the doors.
◆ Clamp the door face-down on the work surface, protecting it with wood pads.
◆ Take a Eurohinge apart and position the boss section in its hole in the door. Check with a carpenter's square that the outside edges of the hinge section and door are parallel to each other.
◆ Mark the holes, drill pilot holes for the screws provided at the marks, then fasten the hinge section to the door *(left)*.
◆ Fasten another boss section to the door at the other end.

2. Attaching the hinges to the cabinets.
◆ Lay the cabinet on the side to which the door will be attached. Reassemble the hinges *(Step 3)* and position the door on the unit in the open position, placing the hinge plate against the cabinet side. Mark the center of the oblong screw holes.
◆ Remove the door and drill pilot holes for the screws provided at the marks.
◆ Take the hinges apart again and fasten the hinge plates to the cabinet side, keeping them perpendicular to the bottom of the cabinet with a carpenter's square *(right)*.

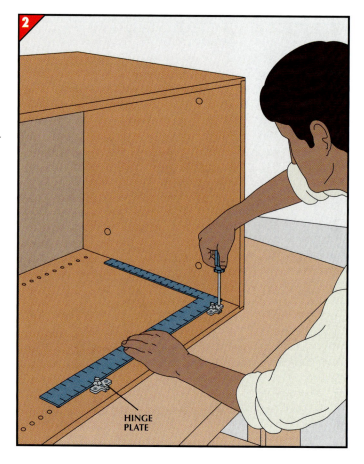

3. Adjusting the door.

◆ Reassemble the hinges by slipping the connector arms of the boss section into the hinge plate.
◆ Close the door and check its alignment. You can adjust the door up or down by loosening the hinge-plate screws and moving the plates; or sideways by moving the hinge arm in or out, or by turning the adjustment screws on the arm itself.

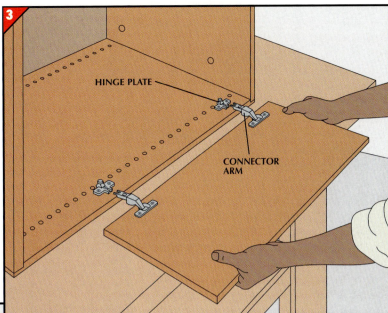

4. Attaching drawer glides to the units.

◆ With the cabinet still on its side, insert the top drawer, leaving enough clearance between the top of the drawer and the cabinet, using a spacer if necessary, so the top edge of the false drawer front *(Steps 5 and 6)* will sit $\frac{1}{8}$ inch below the top of the cabinet.
◆ Mark a line along the bottom edge of each drawer runner *(left)*.
◆ Remove the drawer and fasten the glides to the cabinet sides so their bottom edges are flush with the lines.

5. Measuring for the false front.

◆ Set the cabinet upright and slide in the drawer.
◆ Measure from the outside of the cabinet to the outside of the drawer *(right)*. Transfer the measurement to each end of the false front *(Step 6)*, marking guidelines across the inside face.

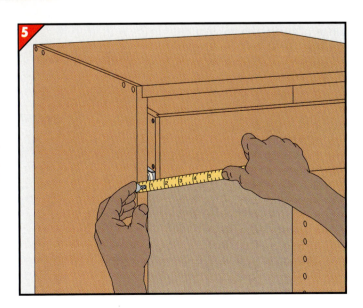

6. Attaching the false front.

◆ Set the false front face-down on the work surface and position the drawer on top between the guidelines so the drawer glides are slightly inset from the bottom edge of the false front.
◆ Measure from the top of the drawer to the top of the false front at each end to ensure the drawer is square to the front, then clamp the assembly in place, protecting the drawer with wood pads.
◆ Drill two pilot holes for 1¼-inch No. 8 wood screws through the drawer front and into the false front, then drive screws *(right)*. Instead of standard screws, you can use adjustable fasteners *(photograph)*, which have plastic nuts that allow the false front to be moved up to 5 mm vertically or horizontally after the pilot holes are drilled and before the fastener is driven. These fasteners require pilot holes that are 20 mm in diameter and 10.5 mm deep.

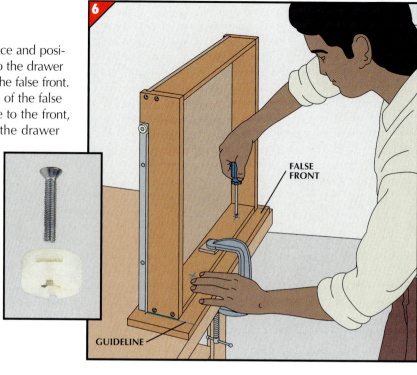

7. Installing the drawer handles.

◆ Measure the width and height of the false front to determine its center.
◆ Clamp the drawer down again with a scrap panel under the false front, then mark the centerpoint on the back of the drawer front with a combination square *(left)*.
◆ At the mark, drill a hole for the screw provided through the drawer front and false front.
◆ Fasten the handle to the drawer.

8. Attaching door handles.

◆ Remove the door from the cabinet and lay it face-down on a scrap panel on the work surface.
◆ With a combination square, mark intersecting lines 3 inches from the bottom and outer side of the door.
◆ Drill a hole for the screw provided through the door at the point where the lines intersect *(right)*, and fasten the handle to the door.

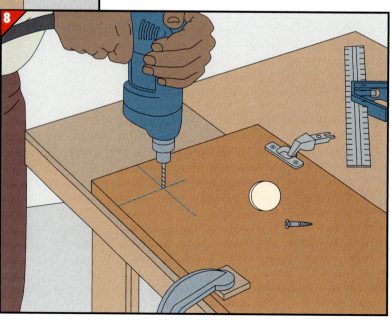

MOUNTING WALL CABINETS

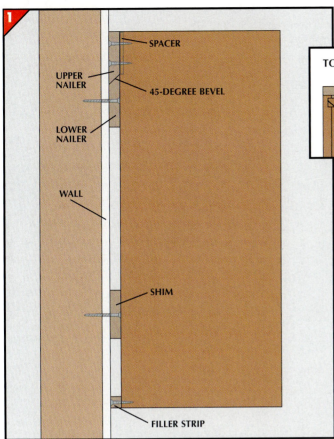

1. A cabinet installation.
Wall cabinets are secured by interlocking nailers, one fastened to the back of each unit and one to the wall. Cut from a single 1-by-6, ripped down the middle at a 45-degree angle, the nailers are not fastened together; however, the cut edges, when put back together, form a solid anchoring system for the cabinets and facilitate removal of the units. Because the back is recessed, a $\frac{1}{4}$-inch plywood spacer is attached to the back of the cabinet along the top edge so the nailer can be mounted flush against the back of the unit. A 1-by-3 shim attached to the wall 3 inches above the bottom of the cabinets and a 1-by-1 filler strip fastened to the units along the bottom hold them plumb.

2. Making the anchoring system.
◆ Referring to your kitchen layout *(pages 17-18)*, snap a level chalk line on the wall at the height of the top of the wall cabinets. Snap a second line $5\frac{1}{2}$ inches below the first, a third where the cabinet bottoms will be, and a fourth 3 inches higher.
◆ Cut a 1-by-6, a 1-by-3, and a 1-by-1 to the length of the cabinet run. Make a 45-degree bevel cut down the middle of the 1-by-6 on a table saw. Fasten half of the board as a nailer to every wall stud with a 3-inch No. 8 wood screw so the uncut edge aligns with the second chalk line.
◆ Fasten the 1-by-3 as a shim to the wall as you did the nailer, aligning its bottom edge with the last chalk line you snapped *(right)*.

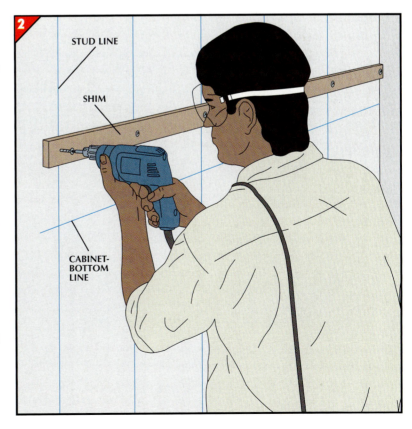

3. Hanging the cabinets.

◆ Make a 3-inch-wide spacer as long as the width of the recessed back from $\frac{1}{4}$-inch plywood. Glue it in place at the top of the back.
◆ Cut a piece from the remaining half of the 1-by-6 nailer to the width of the first cabinet and position its uncut edge along the top of the cabinet. Drill countersunk pilot holes for $1\frac{3}{4}$-inch No. 8 wood screws through the nailer and spacer into the cabinet's back, making a vertical pair of holes near each side and every 16 inches in between.
◆ Fasten a piece of the cut 1-by-1 as a filler strip along the bottom of the cabinet in the same way, but with only a single row of screws.
◆ Lift the cabinet into position *(right)* and hang the nailer on the unit over the one on the wall.
◆ Hang the remaining wall cabinets, then fasten adjacent cabinets together. For each unit, drill pilot holes for 5-mm bolts through two of the shelf pin holes—one at the top and one at the bottom—into the side of the adjacent cabinet, then make each connection with a bolt, washer, and nut.
◆ Install the shelves and the doors for the cabinets.

A COMMERCIAL WALL-ANCHORING SYSTEM

You can buy commercial hardware to anchor frameless cabinets to the wall with the same flexibility as the system shown on these pages. Instead of interlocking nailers, suspension fittings fastened to the cabinet sides attach to a metal rail screwed to the wall. First, fasten the rail to the wall slightly below the proposed level of the tops of the cabinets. Cut a small notch in each upper corner of the cabinet backs to accommodate the fittings, then attach them to the units. Finally, hang the fittings from the rail. Adjustment screws on the fittings allow you to adjust the cabinets vertically or horizontally, or closer to the wall, after the units have been mounted.

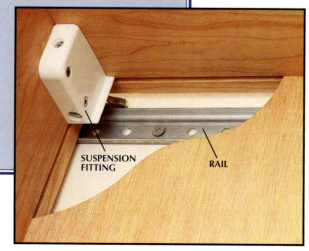

INSTALLING THE BASE UNITS

1. Fastening the base levelers.

◆ Remove any doors or drawers from the cabinet, then lay the unit on one side on a work surface.
◆ Insert a base-leveler bolt and washer into each hole drilled through the bottom panel *(page 115, Step 3)*.
◆ Thread a leveler mounting block onto each bolt.
◆ Tighten the bolts with a socket wrench *(right)* so the flange on each block faces inward.
◆ Slip the leveler legs onto the mounting blocks.

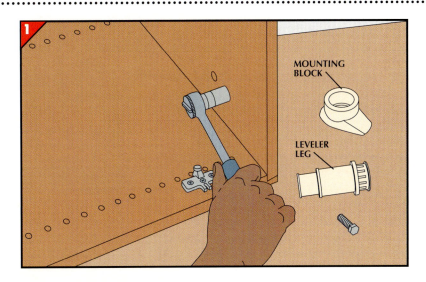

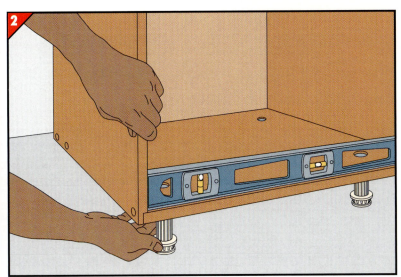

2. Leveling the cabinet.

◆ Working with a helper if necessary, lift the cabinet into place.
◆ Set a carpenter's level across the bottom panel at the front edge of the cabinet and adjust the legs *(left)* as needed until the unit is level.
◆ Place the level along each side panel of the cabinet and adjust the back legs.

3. Attaching kick plates.

◆ For each cabinet side that will be visible, cut a kick plate to reach from the bottom to the floor.
◆ Mark a center line across the plate's inside face, position the plate, and mark the locations of the levelers on the line.
◆ Fasten a mounting plate to the kick plate at each mark with the screws provided.
◆ Slip a clip onto each mounting plate and snap the clips around the levelers *(right)*.
◆ Install the remaining cabinets, then fasten adjacent units together *(opposite, Step 3)*.
◆ Install the shelves, drawers, and doors, and add a countertop *(pages 103-107)*.

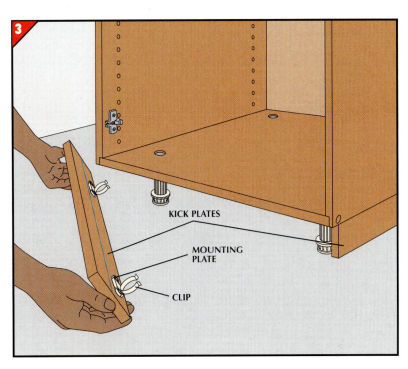

INDEX

AC cable (armored cable): 34, 35
Air gaps for dishwashers: 40
Aluminum-wire safety: 45
Anchoring systems, wall-cabinet: 124
Angle clamps: 117
Armored cable (AC): 34, 35
Asbestos safety: 27

Backsplashes, countertop: 107
Bar hangers for ceiling fixtures: 58
Baseboard trim: 90-93
Bearing vs. nonbearing walls: 26
Bearing walls: removing, 29-32; windows in, 64
Belt sanders: 104
Bits: clutch-driven screwdriver bits, 84; Forstner bits, 108
Boxes. See Outlet boxes
Brick walls: cleaning, 35; cutting, 65-66; exposing, 34-35; mortar joints, patching, 35
Broom closets: 16
Brushes, wire fitting: 23
Building codes: 8

Cabinet designs: 14-19; base cabinets, 14, 15; corner base cabinets, 15; corner wall cabinets, 16; Eurocabinets, 17; face-frame cabinets, 17; filler strips, 14; layouts, 17-18; lazy-susan cabinets, 15; special-use cabinets, 16; wall cabinets, 16. See also Countertops
Cabinets, construction of (Eurocabinets): 108-122; anatomy, 109; assembly, 117-122; cutting, 110-112; drawers, 119, 121-122; drilling, 114, 115; edge banding, 116-117; fasteners, adjustable, 122; handles, 122; hinges, 115, 120-121; jigs, 108; routing dadoes and rabbets, 113
Cabinets, installing (Eurocabinets): 123-125; base cabinets, 125; wall-cabinet anchoring systems, 124; wall cabinets, 123-124
Cabinets, installing (stock cabinets): 96-102; base cabinets, 99-102; wall cabinets, 96-98
Cabinets, removing: 24, 25
Cables. See Wires
C-clamps: 98
Ceiling fixtures, wiring: 53-55, 56-57, 58
Ceiling wallboard, installing: 84
Circuit breakers, wiring: 61
Circuits. See Wiring
Circular saws: 112
Clamps: angle clamps, 117; C-clamps, 98; handscrew clamps, 106; quick-action clamps, 98
Clutch-driven screwdriver bits: 84
Codes: 8
Cooking centers: 10
Coped joints: 93
Coping saws: 93
Corner bead: 85, 86
Countertops: backsplashes, tile, 107; installing, 103-106; removing, 25; types, 15
CPVC (chlorinated polyvinyl chloride) pipes: 36

Dadoes: 113
Designs, kitchen. See Layouts
Dielectric unions: 36
Dimplers: 84
Disabled persons, kitchen designs for: 19
Dishwashers, plumbing for: 39-40
Dowel centers: 114
Dowel jigs: 108, 114
Drawers, cabinet: 119, 121-122
Drill guides: 108
Drip caps: 71, 73

Edge banding: 116-117
Edge-banding trimmers: 117
Edge guides: 112
Electricity: turning off, 22. See also Wiring

Fasteners, adjustable: 122
Fire hazards of aluminum wiring: 45
Fish tape: 48
Fixtures. See Light fixtures
Floors: baseboard trim, 90-93; ceramic tiles, 78-81; squeaky floors, repairing, 33; subfloors, 33
Food-cooking centers: 10
Food-preparation centers: 9
Forstner bits: 108

Galley kitchens: 12
Garbage disposers: 42-43
Gas, turning off: 22
GFCIs (ground-fault circuit interrupters): and aluminum wires, 45; wiring, 51

Handles, cabinet: 122
Handscrew clamps: 106
HEPA filters: 27
Hinge-drilling jigs: 108, 115
Hinges, European: 115, 120-121
Hole-drilling jigs: 108, 114, 115

Ice makers: 41
Islands: 13

Jacks, telescoping: 30
Jigs: cabinet-assembly jigs, 117; edge guides, 112; Eurocabinet construction jigs, 108; hinge-drilling jigs, 108, 115; hole-drilling jigs, 108, 114, 115; pipe-cutting jigs, 39; self-centering dowel jigs, 108, 114; self-centering drill guides, 108; shelf-pin-hole jigs, 115
Joinery: coped joints, 93; scarf joints, 92
Joints, wallboard: 87-89

Laminated veneer lumber (LVL): 26, 29
Layouts: cabinets, 17-18; cooking centers, 10; disabled persons, kitchen designs for, 19; floor tile patterns, 78; food-preparation centers, 9; galley kitchens, 8, 12; islands, 13; L-shaped kitchens, 8, 12; sink centers, 11; special-needs kitchens, 19; triangle concept, 8, 12-13; U-shaped kitchens, 8, 13
Lazy-susan cabinets: 15
Lead safety: 27
Light fixtures: bar hangers for ceiling fixtures, 58; outlet-box types, 47; recessed lighting, installing, 56-57; wiring ceiling boxes, 53-55, 58; wiring three-way lighting schemes, 53-55
Lintels: 65-67
L-shaped kitchens: 12
LVL (laminated veneer lumber): 26, 29

Masonry saws, gas-powered: 65
Masonry techniques: bricklaying, 67; brick walls, clean-

126

ing, 35; brick walls, cutting, 65-66; brick walls, removing plaster from, 34-35; lintels, 65-67; mortar joints, patching, 35; tile flooring, 78-81; weep holes, 67
Molding. *See* Trim
Mortar joints, patching: 35
Muriatic acid: 34, 35

Nonbearing *vs.* bearing walls: 26
Nonbearing walls, removing: 27-29

Outlet boxes: armored cable loops, 49; installing, in brick walls, 34, 35; installing, in wallboard, 44, 48; types, 47; wiring, 49-55, 58

Pantries: 16
Permits: 8
Pipe-cutting jigs: 39
Pipe materials: 36. *See also* Plumbing
Plaster, removing, from brick walls: 34-35
Plumber's torches: 36
Plumbing: dielectric unions, 36; dishwashers, 39-40; garbage disposers, 42-43; ice makers, 41; pipe layouts, 36; pipe materials, 36; refrigerator ice makers, 41; sinks, 23, 24, 37-39; tapping into supply lines, 36-37; valves, saddle shutoff, 41; valves, water shutoff, 23; water, turning off, 23
Preparation centers: 9
PVC (polyvinyl chloride) pipes: 36

Quick-action clamps: 98

Rabbets: 113
Random-orbit sanders: 106
Range hoods: 75-77
Ranges: connecting, to a new subpanel, 59; wiring range receptacles, 51
Receptacles: outlet-box types, 47; wiring end-of-the-run receptacles, 50; wiring GFCIs, 51; wiring middle-of-the-run receptacles, 50; wiring range receptacles, 51
Refrigerator ice makers: 41
Roller stands: 111
Routing: 113

Safety precautions: aluminum wiring, 45; asbestos, 27; lead, 27
Sanders: belt sanders, 104; random-orbit sanders, 106
Saws: circular saws, 112; coping saws, 93; gas-powered masonry saws, 65; table saws, 110, 111
Scarf joints: 92
Self-centering dowel jigs: 108, 114
Self-centering drill guides: 108
Shelf-pin-hole jigs: 115
Siding, cutting: 64, 76
Sink centers (layouts): 11
Sinks: dishwashers, 39-40; garbage disposers, 42-43; plumbing for, 37-39; removing, 24; valves, water shutoff, 23
Squeaky floors, repairing: 33
Subfloors: 33
Subpanels, installing: 59-61
Switches: outlet-box types, 47; wiring middle-of-the-run switches, 52; wiring switch loops, 52; wiring three-way lighting schemes, 53-55

Table saws: 110, 111
Taping joints: 87-89
Telescoping jacks: 30
Tile, ceramic: backsplashes, 107; flooring, 78-81, 91
Tile cutters: 81
Torches, plumber's: 36
Triangle concept: 8, 12-13
Trim: baseboard molding, vinyl, 90; baseboard molding, wood, 91-93; brickmold, 74; coped joints, 93; scarf joints, 92; window trim, 74

U-shaped kitchens: 13

Valves: saddle shutoff valves, 41; water shutoff valves, 23

Wallboard. *See* Walls, interior, restoring
Walls, brick: cleaning, 35; cutting, 65-66; exposing, 34-35; mortar joints, patching, 35
Walls, exterior: cutting, for range hoods, 76; cutting, for windows, 64-66
Walls, interior, removing: 26-32; asbestos safety, 27; bearing *vs.* nonbearing walls, 26; bearing walls, 29-32; lead safety, 27; nonbearing walls, 27-29; utilities, removing, 26, 27
Walls, interior, restoring: 82-93; baseboard trim, 90-93; ceiling wallboard, 84; corner bead, 85, 86; joint compound, applying, 86-89; taping joints, 87-89; wallboard, installing, 82-85
Water: turning off, 23. *See also* Plumbing
Weep holes: 67
Wheelchair access, kitchen designs for: 19
Windows: casement windows, installing, 68-71; energy efficiency, 68, 72; opening walls, 64-67; tall windows between studs, installing, 72-74; trim, 74; types, 68
Wire fitting brushes: 23
Wires: aluminum-wire safety, 45; cable, armored, 34, 35; cable selection, 44; connecting solid wires, 46; connecting stranded wires, 47; insulation, stripping, 46; removing, from brick and plaster walls, 34; removing, from within walls, 26, 27; running cable, 48-49; sheathing, removing, 45; stripping, 45, 46
Wiring: ceiling boxes, 53-55, 58; electricity, turning off, 22; garbage disposers, 43; GFCI receptacles, 51; GFCIs and aluminum wiring, 45; kitchen circuits, 44; lighting schemes, three-way, 53-55; load calculation, 45; outlet boxes, 49-55, 58; range hoods, 77; receptacles, 50-51; recessed lighting, 56-57; running cable, 48-49; subpanels, 59-61; switches, 52-55

Time-Life Books is a division of Time Life Inc.

TIME LIFE INC.
PRESIDENT and CEO: George Artandi

TIME-LIFE BOOKS
PRESIDENT: Stephen R. Frary
PUBLISHER/MANAGING EDITOR: Neil Kagan

**HOME REPAIR AND IMPROVEMENT:
Kitchen Renovations**
EDITOR: Lee Hassig
DIRECTORS OF MARKETING:
  Steven Schwartz, Wells P. Spence
Art Director: Kate McConnell
Associate Editor/Research and Writing:
  Karen Sweet
Editorial Assistant: Patricia D. Whiteford

Director of Finance: Christopher Hearing
Directors of Book Production:
  Marjann Caldwell, Patricia Pascale
Director of Operations: Betsi McGrath
Director of Photography and Research:
  John Conrad Weiser
Director of Editorial Administration:
  Barbara Levitt
Production Manager: Marlene Zack
Quality Assurance Manager: James King
Library: Louise D. Forstall

ST. REMY MULTIMEDIA INC.
President: Pierre Léveillé
Vice President, Finance: Natalie Watanabe
Managing Editor: Carolyn Jackson
Managing Art Director: Diane Denoncourt
Production Manager: Michelle Turbide

Staff for *Kitchen Renovations*

Series Editors: Marc Cassini, Heather Mills
Art Director: Robert Paquet
Assistant Editor: James Piecowye
Designers: Jean-Guy Doiron, Robert Labelle
Photographer: Robert Chartier
Editorial Assistant: George Zikos
Coordinator: Dominique Gagné
Copy Editor: Judy Yelon
Indexer: Linda Cardella Cournoyer
Systems Director: Edward Renaud
Technical Support: Jean Sirois
Other Staff: Normand Boudreault,
  Lorraine Doré, Solange Laberge,
  Francine Lemieux, Jenny Meltzer,
  Brian Parsons, Rebecca Smollett

PICTURE CREDITS
Cover: Photograph, Robert Chartier.
  Art, Robert Paquet.

Illustrators: Gilles Beauchemin, George Bell,
  Frederic F. Bigio from B-C Graphics,
  William J. Hennessy, Walter Hilmers Jr.
  from HJ Commercial Art, Joan McGurren,
  Jacques Perrault, Eduino J. Pereira

Photographers: **End papers:** Glenn Moores
  and Chantal Lamarre. **15:** Robert
  Chartier. **23:** Glenn Moores and Chantal
  Lamarre. **30, 36, 47, 48, 49:** Robert
  Chartier. **65:** Stihl Ltd. **71, 84, 98, 108,
  117, 122:** Glenn Moores and Chantal
  Lamarre. **124:** Robert Chartier.

ACKNOWLEDGMENTS
The editors wish to thank the following individuals and institutions: Anaheim Manufacturing, Anaheim, CA; Bonneville Windows and Doors, Sainte-Marie Beauce, Que.; Broan Manufacturing Co., Inc., A Division of Nortek Inc., Hartford, WI; Theresa Dagenhart, Long's Corporation, Fairfax, VA; Jon Eakes, Montreal, Que.; Endicott Clay Products Co., Fairbury, NE; Euro Ltd., High Point, NC; General Cable Corp., Highland Heights, KY; Louis V. Genuario, Genuario Construction Co., Inc., Alexandria, VA; Jameco Industries Inc., Wyandanch, NY; Marvin Windows and Doors, St. Paul, MN; Milwaukee Tool and Equipment Co., Milwaukee, WI; Nutone Inc., Cincinnati, OH; Richelieu Hardware Ltd., Montreal, Que.; Stihl Ltd., London, Ont.; Tool Trend Ltd., Concord, Ont.; Wolfcraft Inc., Itasca, IL

©1998 Time-Life Books. All rights reserved. No part of this book may be reproduced in any form or by any electronic or mechanical means, including information storage and retrieval devices or systems, without prior written permission from the publisher, except that brief passages may be quoted for reviews.
First printing. Printed in U.S.A.
Published simultaneously in Canada.
School and library distribution by Time-Life Education, P.O. Box 85026, Richmond, Virginia 23285-5026.

TIME-LIFE is a trademark of Time Warner Inc. U.S.A.

**Library of Congress
Cataloging-in-Publication Data**
Kitchen renovations / by the editors of
  Time-Life Books.
p. cm. — (Home repair and improvement)
Includes index.
ISBN 0-7835-3921-5
1. Kitchens—Remodeling—Amateurs'
  manuals.
I. Time-Life Books. II. Series.
TH4816.3.K58K5822   1998
643'.4—dc21   98-13988